D1419430

THE GOLFER'S MANUAL

THE QUINTESSENTIAL GUIDE TO RULES, SCORING, HANDICAPPING AND ETIQUETTE.

——— UPDATED EDITION ———

Paige Warr

THE GOLFER'S MANUAL

The quintessential guide to rules, scoring, handicapping and etiquette

Published by:

Pitch Publishing (Brighton) Ltd, 10 Beresford Court,
Somerhill Road, Hove BN3 1RH
Email: info@pitchpublishing.co.uk
Web: www.pitchpublishing.co.uk

First published 2004
Reprinted and published in hardback 2007

 A catalogue record for this book is available from the British Library.

ISBN 978-1-905411-13-9 Hardback edition
ISBN 978-1-905411-11-5 2nd edition
(ISBN 978-0954246051 1st edition)

Illustrations: Anna Marsh
Cover image: Action Images (PB), Anna Marsh (HB)
Editor: Roy Chuter
Design: Swallow Company

Printed and bound in Great Britain by The Cromwell Press

CONTENTS

Grateful thanks...

To Vicky - for patience, support and typing skills
To Michael and Andy Ellis - for the initial inspiration
To Adrian and Justin, Rex and Bruce, Pat and Tony - for all their help and contributions
To Pitch, my publishers - for their belief and encouragement

PREFACE

This book is a guide to golfing beginners, and of interest to all amateur golfers of any age.

It is intended to give information to everyone and anyone who might be interested in golf, and to encourage them to become more involved in the sport, using the confidence that their new-found knowledge will give them.

This book answers those "what...?" questions. For lessons on "how to play golf", a visit to the PGA Professional is still essential.

An ideal present, therefore, for any golfer who needs a quick reference book and a guide to most aspects of the game.

ETIQUETTE
RULES
HANDICAPPING
SCORING

AND MUCH MORE

INTRODUCTION

Golf is truly an international sport, being played in most countries of the world. Indeed, it may be said to be an interplanetary sport, with Apollo 14 astronaut Alan Shepard having taken two golf balls and a 6 iron to the Moon in 1971. In November 2006 Mikhail Tyurir hit a golf ball into space from the International Space Station.

One of the sport's attractions is, of course, that it can be played by men and women of all ages, from roughly 7 years old (Tiger Woods started even younger) to 90 and beyond. How pleasing it is to see youngsters being given lessons and suddenly finding they are 16 years old, 6 feet tall and hitting the ball out of sight. At the other end of the scale is the ticklish problem of trying to 'play to one's age'. A 65-year-old, for instance, would have to have a handicap of 7 and play to par (on a par 72 course), or shoot a gross 80 with a handicap of 15, to score his age.

An old adage says that we learn something new every day - another that we are never too old to learn. By referring to this book, I trust that you will learn something new, no matter how many years young you may be.

My intention is not to try and take the place of accepted authorities in the sport, but to make golf and its fine practices, procedures and traditions more understandable to all – especially beginners – through being better informed.

DISCLAIMER - Readers should note that nothing contained in this book is intended to supersede, take precedence over or usurp any official publication issued by any of golf's governing bodies in any country. Readers should refer to official publications for final 'chapter and verse' on all matters such as rules, decisions on the rules, local rules, organisation of competitions, etc.

Gender – Players are referred to in the 'male' gender throughout (as in the RULES OF GOLF) for brevity and clarity, but all references are intended to apply equally to female players.

Left-handed Players - The text refers to right-handed players, but the opposite will apply to left-handed players.

SECTION 1

BEFORE YOU REACH THE FIRST TEE

A Background to World Golf; Organisations in the UK; Joining a Club; Dress code and Etiquette; People and Places; Introduction to the Rules; Equipment.

A BACKGROUND TO WORLD GOLF

1.00. History

Vast libraries have been devoted to the origins of golf – but who did invent the game? Arguments have raged for many years, with claims by various continental countries, especially the Netherlands where 'kolf' was played in the 15th century. However, it is generally accepted by the world at large that the game as we know it today started with 'gowf' in Scotland. The 'home' of golf is The Royal and Ancient Golf Club of St Andrews, Fife, Scotland, UK, usually abbreviated to the R&A.

1.01. Professional v Amateur

Professional golfers in the UK belong to the Professional Golfers Association (PGA) and to the USPGA in America. Golfers earn their livings from

golf through prize monies won, sponsorship, appearance fees, corporate lessons etc. Very often rules, modes of play and other facets of the game are adapted to suit tournament conditions and other requirements of the professional game, but the changes do not apply to the amateur sport.

Amateur golfers play the game as a non-remunerative and non-profit-making sport. They do not receive payment for teaching golf. They are bound by the Rules of Amateur Status, as approved by the Royal and Ancient Golf Club of St Andrews (R&A Rules Ltd) and the United States Golf Association, and their governing body in any country will be the national union of that country.

All amateur golfers must be aware of the definition of prize vouchers, retail value of prizes, symbolic prizes, hole-in-one prizes, testimonial awards and allowable expenses. Prize money must not exceed certain limits (£500 in Europe, as of 1 January 2004). A player who breaches the RULES OF AMATEUR STATUS as defined in the RULES OF GOLF (see 1.31) may forfeit his amateur status.

"*If in doubt – check it out*"

1.02. World Organisation

For the professional golfer the World is divided into Tours. The two premier Tours are the American and the European, whilst other Tours include the Asian, South African, Japanese and Australasian. A professional golfer may play on any Tour, subject to prior qualification and the obtaining of a tour card, which can be withdrawn if required standards or earnings are not met.

Usually, an aspiring professional will play on a junior tour first, e.g. the Buy.com in the USA or the Challenge Tour in the U.K. There is also an annual qualifying 'Q' school in the USA and Europe, where candidates can seek to qualify (the top 35 or so receive their Tour cards). Ladies and Seniors (50+) have similar Tours.

1.03 . The Majors

Whilst each Tour will have a continuing programme of events each year, there are four championships that are considered to be more important than all others. These are:

- The Masters (played at Augusta, Georgia)
- The US Open
- The Open Championship (played in England or Scotland)
- The USPGA Championship

To win all four in one year would be called the Grand Slam of golf. Amateurs may seek to qualify for entrance.

1.04. The World Championships

Three events are held each year. They are:

- February - accenture Match Play Championship
- March - ca Championship
- July - Bridgestone Invitational

1.05. The Ryder Cup and other professional international competitions

First contested in 1927, the Ryder Cup is an event played every two years between two teams of professional golfers, representing the USA and Europe. Each side takes it in turn to host the event, usually in September. The 2008 event takes place at Valhalla GC, Kentucky and will move to Wales in 2010, Illinois in 2012 and Scotland in 2014.

A similar event, called the President's Cup, is held in alternating years, with the USA taking on an International Team (excluding Europe).

Other events include the Warburg Cup for Seniors (over 50s), the UBS Cup (over 40s), and the Solheim Cup for Ladies (USA v Europe).

1.06. The Walker Cup (men) and Curtis Cup (ladies)

The Walker Cup is played, every two years, between

a team of amateur golfers from the USA, and their counterparts from Great Britain and Ireland. Each side takes it in turn to host the event. The Curtis Cup is also played every two years involving teams of amateur ladies fielded by the USA, and Great Britain with Ireland.

Many other International amateur events, including some for juniors, take place each year.

ORGANISATIONS IN THE UK

1.07. Council of National Golf Unions (CONGU)

CONGU, established in 1960, is the central body of the Men's Golf Unions, which administer the Standard Scratch Score and Handicapping Scheme. They also make recommendations regarding the allocation of stroke indices (see 2.09) for the English Golf Union, the Golfing Union of Ireland, the Scottish Golf Union, the Welsh Golfing Union, and the R&A.

1.08. Golf Unions

Golf Unions for men are formed on a County or Area basis. They are involved in all aspects of amateur golf, acting as authorities for determining all questions which may arise, and generally promoting the welfare and interests of their affiliated (EGU) members. They organise matches with other Counties, County Golf Championships, and competitions. They maintain a uniform system of handicapping, and liaise with the R&A and other organisations through EGU. They are non-profit-making organisations.

1.09. English Golf Union (EGU)

The English Golf Union, based at Woodhall Spa, was established in 1924. It is the governing body for men's amateur golf in England. Its main aims are to allow groups to form societies in the correct manner, to give them credibility and education and to allow easier access to affiliated golf courses. It arranges amateur tournaments and looks after the interests of affiliated Golf Clubs and Club Members.

1.10. The National Golf Centre

The National Golf Centre, home of the EGU, is based at Woodhall Spa, Lincolnshire LN10 6PU.

1.11. Ladies Golf Union (LGU)

The LGU, based at St Andrews, is the governing body for Ladies' golf in Great Britain and Ireland. It consists of four National bodies representing England, Ireland, Scotland and Wales. Until 2004, the LGU handicapping system was delegated to each national organisation. From that year, it was unified with the men's handicapping system under CONGU. See 2.05.

The LGU runs the British Championships, and International events including the Weetabix British Women's Open Championship, the Curtis Cup, the British Women's Amateur Championship and the Home Internationals, together with a range of services to women golfers and affiliated Clubs.

1.12. English Ladies Golf Association (ELGA)

ELGA is based in Birmingham, and was founded in 1952. It is the governing body for Ladies' Amateur Golf in England. There are 35 affiliated (LGU) County Associations, which are split into four divisions. The main objectives are to further the interests of women's amateur golf in England, to administer the handicapping system, to run national championships and other competitions, to select England teams, and to use the Association's funds to best advantage.

1.13. England Golf Partnership

The England Golf Partnership is comprised of the EGU, ELGA and the PGA with the support of the Golf Foundation and Sport England. Its aim, through the implementation of its Whole Sport Plan, is to increase and widen the participation levels in golf and achieve a vision of being 'The Leading Golf Nation in the World by 2020' right through to elite level.

1.14. Golf Foundation

The Golf Foundation is a registered charity, established to develop and promote junior golf for boys and girls, throughout Great Britain. It is supported by all the governing bodies of golf, and many companies and individuals. The aims of the Foundation are to provide support and facilities for golf in schools, and to encourage young people to take up the game, thereby developing their skills, improving their understanding of the game, and aiming towards obtaining a handicap. It also provides competitive opportunities for motivated youngsters.

1.15. National Association of Public Golf Courses (NAPGC)

The NAPGC was formed in 1927 on a voluntary basis. It draws its finances from subscriptions paid by Member Clubs and a grant from the EGU. Competitions are financed by entrance fees. Its aim is to unite the clubs formed on public courses in England and Wales and their Course Managements, in the furtherance of the interest of amateur golf. Membership is open to all properly-constituted clubs which play on courses open to the general public, and to their Managements.

1.16. The Golf Secretary

Every Golf Club has a 'Secretary' (sometimes called the Golf Manager in larger Golf & Country Clubs). He is the person responsible for the organisation and day-to-day running of the Club. If you wish to join a golf Club, or enquire about membership, fees, etc, then the Secretary is the person you should contact.

JOINING A GOLF CLUB

1.17. Starting to play golf

Many golfers will begin their playing careers at a pitch-and-putt course or visit a driving range. As they become more proficient, they may seek to play on a

pay-as-you-play or local municipal course (see 1.28). These are all excellent introductions to the sport, and many players will happily continue to play at these locations without ever wishing to join a Members' Club. Those wishing to obtain a handicap may pursue the opportunity outlined in 1.13 or something similar.

If you decide that you wish to join a golf Club, you must obtain an application form from the Secretary, and submit this, usually together with written support from a Proposer and a Seconder (probably Club members). You may be asked to attend an interview. If your application is successful, you may be asked to attend a 'New Members' evening (see also 1.13).

Members will be expected to obtain an official handicap before being allowed to play on the course.

1.18. Member's Subscription

A golf Club normally charges a one-off 'entry' fee, very often equal to one year's membership subscription, and the annual membership subscription itself. This will become more expensive the closer one gets to London, or for a particularly prestigious Club.

1.19. Green Fees

Green fees are what you pay if you wish to play at a Club of which you are not a member, in other words as a visitor. There will be a charge either for one round or for the full day.

1.20. Visitors

If wishing to visit another Club, you are well advised to telephone first and agree a tee time, and determine whether an official handicap certificate is required. You must expect to sign a register and pay green fees. If you are playing with a member of the host club, reduced green fees may be applicable. Societies often negotiate reduced green fees for groups of visitors. Evidence of Club Membership and/or an official handicap is likely to be requested of each player.

1.21. The Professional

The Professional and his staff at a golf Club are responsible for the receipt of green fees, the selling of golf equipment and clothes, and the giving of golf lessons. They are normally located in a 'shop', which is near to or adjoining the Club House, and should be your first port of call.

1.22. Insurance

Golf can be a very dangerous game, either in respect of damage done to yourself by another player, or to another player, third party or property, by you. Normally, the payment of your annual membership subscription, or the payment of a green fee as a visitor, will provide insurance cover for such eventualities. You should, however, make enquiries and satisfy yourself on this point. Many golfers take out private insurance, which can also include loss or damage to golf clubs, etc, especially when abroad.

1.23. Travelling Overseas

Historically, airlines have not charged extra for the carriage of golf bags and clubs. This, however, is changing, and you should make enquiries regarding charging, weight allowed, and excess baggage fees.

Golf bags and clubs are normally to be deposited at a separate designated point in the departure terminal, as directed when you check in. At the destination airport they may appear on the luggage carousel or at a separate pick-up point. It is wise to enquire which it will be.

DRESS CODE AND ETIQUETTE

1.24. How to Dress

Golf has always attached great importance to the wearing of acceptable attire, and the adage that "if you look good, you will feel good and you will play well". (On pay-as-you-play or municipal courses the importance of a strict dress code is reduced. It makes sense, however, to wear appropriate clothes and, above all, spiked golf shoes.) Clubs require certain standards of those playing on their courses, and this applies to both behaviour and apparel.

Generally, the days of plus-fours and jackets have gone, but many golfers still sport plus-twos and woollen caps. There are however, various clothing rules imposed by Clubs, which if not followed will almost certainly prevent you playing.

These may include:

- No trainers - proper golfing shoes with metal spikes or soft spikes - called cleats - must be worn. Kilties, the leather flaps which cover the laces, seem to be going out of fashion.
- No jeans – proper trousers of golf design or otherwise. Never, ever, tuck your trouser bottoms into your socks. Shorts should be tailored, knee length and worn with socks which cover the calf, or at the very least be ankle-length athletic socks.
- No collarless t-shirts – t-shirts should have collars, although some professionals are now wearing

round-neck t-shirts or crew-neck jumpers.
- No running shorts.
- No track suits.
- No baseball caps worn back to front.

Cameras and phones should never be taken on to a course, whether you are a spectator or a player. It is also wise to check on a Club's dress code in advance.

1.25. Etiquette

A French word, it means behaviour or courtesy.

Section 1 of the RULES OF GOLF has been enhanced as of the 1 January 2004 edition, and now includes the Spirit of the Game, safety, consideration of other players, pace of play, priority on the course, care of the course, and penalties for breach of the guidelines.

You are recommended to read Section 1 of the RULES OF GOLF and practice the guidelines set out therein. See also 2.16.

Good behaviour is a hallmark of golf and should be encouraged at all times. Particular attention should be given to standing perfectly still and maintaining absolute quiet when another player is taking a stance and playing a stroke. A player should avoid advancing up the fairway in advance of another's unplayed ball, which, apart from the lack of courtesy, is dangerous. Special care should be taken on the greens and in bunkers. Do not run on a course, and do not vent your anger, whether verbally or physically. Golf should be played with dignity and respect for others.

So important is etiquette that pointers to it are liberally splashed around this book.

PEOPLE AND PLACES

1.26. The Starter

Not all clubs have a starter, but when one is present he will be located in a 'Starter's hut' near the first tee. He is responsible for ensuring that players play from the first tee at the booked, or pre-arranged tee time as shown on the tee sheet, and that players are properly attired and visitors have paid their green fees. Where no starter is present, the Professional or his staff will perform these duties. If, however, a starter is on duty, you must report to him or her before approaching the first tee. The Professional will advise.

1.27. The Greenkeepers

Courses are maintained by the Head Greenkeeper and his staff (Superintendents in the USA). Players, however, should take every opportunity to protect the course by using divot mix where provided, replacing divots, raking bunkers, and repairing pitchmarks on greens. Always ensure that you obey directions on the course indicated by ropes or signs, e.g. 'Players this way'. This ensures that the very wet or worn areas under repair have every opportunity to regrow. Greenkeepers will be aware that rabbits tend to 'scrape' on bare areas, and will therefore try to encourage grass growth wherever possible.

1.28. Municipal Courses

In many areas there are municipal golf courses, as opposed to private members' clubs. They are normally owned, managed, and maintained by the Local Authority or a private company. Some may be 9 holes only, and some are made up solely of Par 3 holes.

Most are open to anyone, with or without an official handicap, on a pay-as-you-play basis. They are excellent for beginners, who are thus able to experience the sport before committing to a substantial financial outlay. Seasoned players may also prefer to play on a pay-as-you-play basis. See 1.13 and 1.15 to find out about the organisations supporting municipal courses.

1.29. Driving Ranges

Driving ranges are private facilities where any aspiring golfer may practise his swing under cover without having to collect the balls afterwards! Many golfers use the facility on a regular basis. Payment at the office produces a token to be used in a machine in order to receive a bucket of golf balls. Remember to put the empty bucket in place before pressing in the token, or you will be surrounded by golf balls, much to the amusement of your friends!

1.30. Practice Grounds

Practice grounds are open areas attached to many golf courses where players can go to practise. They must provide their own balls and collect them afterwards.

INTRODUCTION TO THE RULES

1.31. The Rules of Golf

The Rules of Golf Committee of the R&A was formed in 1897 to produce a single code of rules for the game of golf. 127 countries, associations and unions,

worldwide, are affiliated to the R&A and accept the Club's authority over the laws of the game, whilst the USA, Canada and Mexico - where the Rules are set by the USGA - have their own Rules body. All players should obtain a **free** copy of the current "RULES OF GOLF" (ROG) as approved by The Royal and Ancient Golf Club of St Andrews, and the United States Golf Association.

From 1 January 2004, the R&A transferred to R&A Rules Ltd the responsibilities and authority of the R&A in making, interpreting and giving decisions on the RULES OF GOLF.

Changes to the previous RULES OF GOLF introduced at this time include:

- A definition of the 'Spirit of the Game'.
- The disqualification of offenders for bad behaviour.
- Limits on drivers (appendix II).
- The removal of loose impediments on the green (Rule 16.1.a).
- The withdrawal of Rule 18.2.c and the amendment of Rule 23.1, dealing with the removal of loose

impediments other than on the green.

- Marking of ball position for 'preferred lies' – a Specimen Local Rule is listed in ROG Appendix I, part B, 3b.

Disabled golfers should obtain the R&A publication entitled 'A Modification of the Rules of Golf for Golfers with Disabilities'.

Readers should note that ROG is updated every four years (last revision 1 January 2004), and can be obtained easily. Nothing in this book in any way supersedes, replaces or should influence the text or intention of the RULES OF GOLF.

Disputes over rules are a common topic of conversation after a round. Many golfers become very interested in the rules and take part in local and national rules quizzes. All golfers should become acquainted with the rules to ensure fair competition and avoidance of penalties. Rule 6-1 states that a player is responsible for knowing the Rules.

There are thirty-four rules in RULES OF GOLF (Rule

35 is the name of a golf ball) but there are very many sections and subsections. Apart from the Rules of Play contained in Section III, the RULES OF GOLF also contains a Foreword; How to use the Rule Book; Principal Changes (from the last edition); Section I Etiquette; Section II Definitions; and three Appendices covering (I) Local Rules, (II) design of clubs, and (III) the ball. There are notes relating to handicaps and Rules of Amateur Status.

Note: Rule 1-3 states that players shall not agree to exclude the operation of any Rule or to waive any penalty incurred. In competition, the penalty for breach of this Rule is disqualification. You have been warned!

1.32. Decisions on the Rules of Golf 2006 - 2007

'DECISIONS ON THE RULES OF GOLF' is produced by R&A Rules Ltd and the United States Golf Association (2006 - £14.99). It was first published in Great Britain in 1998, in order to clarify matters that might otherwise be ambiguous and to stem the flow of written requests (about 3,000 per year) sent to the R&A. It is a most interesting companion to the RULES OF GOLF and will give the reader many hours of enjoyable, and often amusing, reading in addition to providing answers to those convoluted questions that occur wherever golf is played. The last update was published in 2006, with the next scheduled for 2008.

Amongst other changes the 2006 - 2007 edition allows Clubs to make a Local Rule to permit the use of distance measuring instruments and also help players who have signed for the correct score on the wrong scorecard.

1.33. Local Rules

The Committee of any Golf Club may make and publish Local Rules for local abnormal conditions if they are consistent with the policy set forth in Appendix 1 of the RULES OF GOLF. Part B gives specimen Local Rules. In addition, detailed information regarding acceptable and prohibited

Local Rules is provided in 'Decisions on the Rules of Golf.' (See 1.32). Any proposed modification of a Rule of Golf must be authorised by R & A Rules Ltd.

Local rules are printed on the back of scorecards provided by every Club or course and may concern items as the removal of stones in bunkers, paths and walkways not integral parts of the course, intervening sprinkler heads near greens, and shelters as immovable obstructions.

1.34. Lessons

Before being allowed on to a Members' Golf Course, it will be necessary to produce evidence of previous membership at a Club and/or an official handicap certificate (see 1.13). Beginners should take lessons with the Professional, and will usually be required to play part of the course with the Professional before a provisional handicap is awarded and permission given to play. Most golfers will continue to have lessons or coaching throughout their playing careers.

1.35. Grip

The connection between the player and his club is called the 'grip' and is of fundamental importance.

Basically there are three grips:

- The overlapping – most favoured
- The Interlocking – preferred by people with small hands.
- The Baseball – not advocated because the hands do not act as one.

Most right-handed golfers wear a glove on their left hand, which is said to strengthen the grip. It is not essential. Gloves of special materials may aid golfers in wet playing conditions. Hand warmers and large gloves for both hands are available for colder climes.

A 'strong' grip is one where the right hand (for right-handed players) is almost under the club-shaft and the player at the address position can see three or four knuckles of the left hand; a draw or hook may result. A 'weak' grip is when the left hand is under the club-shaft and three or four knuckles of the right hand are seen by the player at the address position (see Glossary) – a fade or slice may result.

When referring to a golf club, the 'grip' is the rubber, or similar material, fixed to the club-shaft and immediately in contact with the golfer's hands. The grips on all clubs should be kept clean and feel 'tacky'. If they feel 'slippery', they can easily be replaced by the Club Professional.

1.36. Tempo

Professional golfers are envied for the tempo of their swings. A club has to be swung backwards and then forwards in one movement. Do not try to 'hit' the ball; rather let the ball get in the way of the clubface. Essentially, the club must be accelerating when it strikes the ball and the whole process must result in a balanced posture when completed. The club speed at each part of the swing, therefore, produces a tempo to achieve an optimum performance. Lessons with the Club Professional will begin this process.

1.37. Clubs

The design of clubs is covered in Appendix II of the RULES OF GOLF with diagrams showing heel, toe, face, sole, etc.

To non-golfers, or golf beginners, the clubs used by players can be a mystery. Woods are no longer made of wood, irons are not made of iron.

A wood is a club, usually used off the tee or fairway, to hit long distances. Originally, the head was made of persimmon wood (hence the name) and the shaft of hickory with a leatherbound grip.

Technology has changed everything, and continues to do so. The head is now commonly made of metal (usually titanium), although there was a phase of wood combined with metal. Shafts – maximum length 48 inches – are made of steel or graphite

(carbon, or similar), with grips made of various combinations of rubber. When a shaft appears through the soleplate, this is called 'bore-through' and is said to reduce twisting at impact.

The size of a driver's head is measured in cubic centimetres, being the volume of water displaced when the head is immersed. The size of a clubhead must not exceed 460cc, plus a tolerance of 10cc, making the maximum 470cc. In 2007, square-headed drivers were introduced.

Coefficient of Restitution (COR) refers to the 'trampolining' effect of a club's face: it is the subject of controversy. A worldwide standard for all drivers, limiting COR to 0.83, comes into effect in 2008.

The EGU banned non-conforming drivers (those with a maximum 'characteristic time' exceeding 257 microseconds) for certain competitions from 1 January 2005. Top amateurs only need check.

Woods are numbered 1 to 11, although 1 (the 'driver' off the tee), 2, 3 and 4 are commonest. 5, 7 and 9 are becoming commoner and often preferred by ladies.

'*Rescue*' clubs, sometimes called 'recovery' or 'utility' clubs, are a combination of a wood and an iron. They have a loft of between 18° and 24° and are generally used in place of a 3-iron.

An *iron* has a head commonly made of forged and/or cast steel. The head may be 'blade' shaped or have a 'progressive cavity' back with peripheral weighting. Again, shafts are metal or graphite (carbon or similar). Irons are numbered 1 to 9, with 1 hitting the longest distance and 9 the shortest. 1 and 2 are usually only used by professional players.

The lie angle of a club - the angle between ground and shaft - will vary from 58° for an iron to 66° for a sand wedge. The stiffness or flexibility of a club shaft will vary from extra stiff, through stiff and regular, to flexible. Your Professional will advise on the most suitable shaft for you. See Glossary, Swing weight.

Wedges are iron clubs, consisting of pitching wedges for approach play and sand irons for very short shots or getting out of bunkers. A sand iron (or sand wedge) has a very wide sole, which enables it to bounce off the sand in a bunker rather than 'dig in'.

In addition, there are *gap wedges* (between a pitching wedge and a sand iron), and *lob wedges*, which have less 'bounce' than a sand iron, for very high shots. Some wedges are deliberately designed to rust, thus providing more friction between the clubface and the ball. Chippers are sometimes used for putting from off the green. Double-sided chippers are illegal.

Putters are made of various materials and combinations of materials. Designs are very variable and subject to personal taste. Inserts of softer material can be built into the face of the blade, which may also contain ceramics or glass. The face on a 'face-balanced' putter remains horizontal (facing the sky) when the whole club is balanced on one finger, as opposed to being vertical (facing forwards).

The faces of clubs have an angle from the vertical called the loft, measured in degrees. A small loft will keep the ball close to the ground and travel farther. A large loft will send the ball upwards but not so far.

Players should determine through practice and experience how far they actually hit with each club. Figures for average distances are given overleaf.

Club	Ladies Av. yards	Men Av. yards
1W (Driver)	180	220
2W		
3W (Fairway)	170	210
4W		
5W	150	190
6W		
7W	130	170
8W		
9W	110	150
1 Iron*	160	200
2 I *	150	190
3 I	140	180
4 I	130	160
5 I	120	150
6 I	110	140
7 I	100	130
8 I	90	120
9 I	80	110
PW	70	90
SW	60	80
LW	50	70

* *Generally, professionals only*

Lofts for irons vary from 12° for a 1-iron to 64° for a lob wedge, although it depends on the manufacturer.

Most clubs have a pattern on their faces designed to impart backspin on the ball for 'control'. The design of the grooves is carefully specified. See Glossary.

A couple of useful, club-related terms…an 'offset' club is one where the blade is farther behind the line of the shaft than normal – it is said to help reduce a slice. And the 'hosel' is where the shaft joins the clubhead.

Note that for courses at high altitude, the distances achieved with the longer clubs will increase. Low temperatures tend to reduce yardages.

1.38. 'Look-alike' Clubs

Purchasers of golf clubs should be aware that, in addition to clubs with well-known brand names, there are clubs that are sold with the intention of deceiving the purchaser into thinking that they are buying a brand name when in fact it is a copy or imitation. The saving in initial purchase cost may later prove to be illusory. 'Look-alike' clubs may look like, be designed like, or mimic the entire identity of a well-known brand, or may be carbon-copy replicas.

'Look-alike' clubs may, or may not, be legal. They may in fact be perfectly usable and perform well, though materials and finishes may be inferior. Many 'look-alike' clubs originate in China and Taiwan. Watch out for well-known brand names that have been misspelt.

You should be able to tell who makes a club simply by looking at it. A bona-fide product will clearly identify the manufacturer by name and will usually show a corporate logo or trademark.

1.39. Maximum number of clubs

When playing on the golf course a player may carry a maximum of 14 clubs. Penalties are applied if this number is exceeded. Partners may share clubs provided that the total number of clubs carried by the partners so sharing does not exceed fourteen. This usually applies only to foursomes.

Any players contemplating sharing clubs are advised to obtain the Secretary's permission in advance. If you damage a club during the normal course of play you may continue to use it, repair it or replace it. If you damage it for any other reason, e.g. in a fit of temper, then the club shall not be used or replaced.

1.40. First set of clubs

For a novice seeking to acquire their first set of clubs, it may well be that a second-hand set is obtained first. This is very usual, and enables the potential player to have a go before spending a lot of money.

It is not necessary to have 14 clubs from the outset. A starter set – comprising seven or eight clubs and sometimes known as a 'short' or 'half' set – will suffice. This might consist of 3 wood, 4 iron, 6 iron, 8 iron, pitching wedge, sand wedge and putter. Later, a full set might consist of 1 wood, 3 wood, 5 wood, 3 iron, 4 iron, 5 iron, 6 iron 7 iron, 8 iron, 9 iron, pitching wedge, sand iron, lob wedge and putter.

Before buying new clubs, the advice of a Professional should be sought. The Professional will advise on shaft length (depends on height); lie of the head (depends upon arm length); swing weight (depends on body build); shaft material (depends upon age/strength); grip size (depends upon hand size) and other factors. It is a strange piece of trivia that very often a tall man's hands will be exactly the same distance from the floor as a short man's!

Often a 'matching' set (all made by the same manufacturer) may be bought, and whilst this has its attractions, mainly for appearance and consistency, it is not essential.

1.41. Golf Balls

From the top-hatful of feathers squeezed into a leather casing (the feathery introduced in 1618) through the plastic gutta percha (introduced in 1848) and the Haskell one-piece rubber covered ball (adopted in 1901) to the modern day golf ball, technology has transformed the composition and

surface materials completely.

We now have a choice between combinations of two-piece, three-piece, four-piece; soft core, hard core; wound; multi-layer, urethane cover; surlyn cover; high compression; low compression; high trajectory; low trajectory; extra distance; and multiple dimple patterns…to name but a few.

Originally standardised in 1921, the weight of a golf ball shall not be greater than 1.620 ounces. Its diameter used to be 1.620 inches, but since 1990, when the larger American ball was adopted, it is to be not less than 1.680 inches. See Appendix III of the RULES OF GOLF for details.

Generally, a hard ball (compression 100) will have good distance, whilst a soft ball (compression 90) will have greater 'feel' for accurate short play. You will know a 90-compression ball because the maker's name will be in black and the number in red. With 100-compression balls, both are in black.

Professionals usually use golf balls which have a soft

cover for good 'feel'. Nowadays, however, there are many combinations searching for the ultimate in distance, feel, spin and trajectory. See Glossary.

The cost of golf balls varies depending upon the technology involved. Beginners should be content with 'used' balls from the Professional's shop or other retail outlets. Also available are 'lake' balls, which are perfectly good balls dredged from golf course lakes (mainly in America). Eventually, you may alight upon a preferred ball, and henceforth advise friends and family of your choice prior to birthdays and Xmas!

Do not use driving range balls on a golf course.

The 'shelf life' of a golf ball is said to be three years. If your ball feels and sounds like a lump of concrete, then maybe it's too old! Invest in, or find, another one!

Golf balls are historically white in colour but many different colours and patterns can now be obtained. Lime/yellow are good for foggy conditions, whilst orange/red are useful in snow and ice. Pink patterns are also on the market.

A carton of three balls is often called a 'sleeve'.

1.42. Bags, trolleys and buggies

Bags are basically of three main types:-

- Firstly, the 'carry' bag is lightweight, has limited pockets, and usually has a tripod facility in order to stand it clear of the wet ground. Dual shoulder straps are now available.
- The 'normal' bag will carry everything required but usually is carried on a trolley.
- The third type is the 'professional' bag, which is huge and normally carried by a caddie.

There are also pencil bags to hold a few clubs only, and bags for juniors.

Trolleys can either be pulled or be powered by a

battery-driven motor. During inclement weather they may be restricted in which case you will have to carry. Many courses now have buggies, which carry two people and all their golf equipment. Some clubs worldwide (including almost every one in the USA) will insist that buggies are used. Care should be taken to determine whether you may drive the buggy anywhere on the fairways or whether you must keep to purpose-built buggy paths. Many buggies have a 'distance' display showing how far you are from the next green. How's that for unexpected help, or should that be unnecessary help?

Caddies are paid by golfers to carry equipment and give yardages, wind speed and direction, and important information. If you are hiring a caddie, maybe you are already a professional golfer?

SECTION 2

YOU HAVE ARRIVED AT THE FIRST TEE

The Game of Golf; Handicapping; How to score; Forms of competitive play.

You have now read the book, had the lessons, seen the video, been allocated a handicap, obtained a scorecard and are ready to go!

THE GAME OF GOLF

2.00. The Course

You will normally be expected, subject to health, weather, etc, to start at Hole No. 1 and proceed through all 18 holes in their numerical order. It is frowned upon to miss odd holes – far better to play a few holes and then leave the course.

2.01. A Hole

A hole consists of playing your first stroke from a teeing ground (the tee) to a closely mown area called 'the fairway', either side of which may be uncut grass, heather, gorse, etc. called 'the rough'. The ball must be propelled towards the 'putting green' and 'holed out' – the ball must be at rest below the level of the lip of the hole. Along the way, you may encounter various hazards such as water (lakes, rivers, streams etc) and sand bunkers (called traps in America).

Subject to the Rules, each hole should be completed using the same ball between tee and green. Once the ball has been struck on the tee, it is 'in play', and may only be touched or moved in accordance with the RULES OF GOLF. You may change your ball between holes subject to personal identification.

Your score for each hole must be recorded, and a total for all 18 calculated at the end of the round. See also 2.07, Strokeplay, and 2.08, Matchplay.

Note that it is not essential for you to have a personal handicap, score every hole or enter competitions. Golf can be very mathematical, and beginners will be concentrating on how to play, rather than the complexities of handicapping and scoring.

As with any sport, however, 'competition', if only with your friends, will inevitably arise. It is advocated therefore that all players should become familiar with the way handicaps and scores are calculated in order to increase their enjoyment. See 2.05 and 2.10. Most Members' Clubs will insist that a recognised handicap is obtained.

2.02. Par

Every hole has been given a 'par', which is shown on the scorecard obtained from the Professional's Shop before starting. Par is the number of strokes that a reasonably good player should take on each hole.

- Par 3 - normally a short hole not more than about 250 yards. The allowance of three strokes is for one shot between the tee and the green, and then two putts.
- Par 4 - a hole between 250 yards and 475 yards approximately. The allowance of four strokes is one shot from tee to fairway, one shot from fairway to green, and then two putts.
- Par 5 - a long hole normally in excess of 475 yards. The allowance of five strokes is one shot from tee to fairway; one shot from fairway to fairway; one shot from fairway to green, and then two putts.

Note: The yardages for Ladies will be shorter.

Most courses have two Par 3 holes, fourteen Par 4 holes, and two Par 5 holes. The total Par score for the course is thus (2x3=)6 + (14x4=)56 + (2x5=)10 =

72. If the number of Par 3s and Par 5s is the same, the overall par will always be 72.

A player who owned a course was asked the par of a particular hole. "Anything I want it to be," he replied. "Today, it's 12, and I've just birdied the blighter!"

2.03. Standard Scratch Score (SSS)

The system devised to produce fair handicapping between players of different abilities, playing on different courses, involves a rating known as the Standard Scratch Score (SSS).

Introduced in 1926, but since modified, it is, generally speaking, the score that a scratch player (one with a zero handicap) would expect to make on any given course in ideal conditions.

It varies between courses due to factors such as total length, width of fairways, size of greens, amount of bunkering, nearness of out-of-bounds, whether the course is sheltered from prevailing winds and so on.

Handicaps of all players are based on the SSS of their home course. The SSS is an overall course rating and not necessarily a total of the pars of 18 holes.

2.04. Competition Standard Scratch (CSS)

After a competition, when all scores have been recorded, and nett scores – number of strokes taken minus handicap allowance – have been calculated, they are averaged out (thus providing for adverse weather conditions, etc) to arrive at a Competition Standard Scratch (CSS). Anyone achieving that nett score or between one or four strokes above it, depending on category (See 2.05(a) below), will not have their handicaps adjusted. This is known as being in the 'buffer zone' (see Table in 2.05). Those recording more than the four allowed strokes above the CSS will have their handicaps increased by 0.1. Nett scores below the CSS will invoke reductions in handicaps in accordance with the table given in 2.05.

In normal weather you may predict that the CSS will be equal to the par for the course.

2.05. How it works and why it's used

The RULES OF GOLF does not legislate for the allocation or adjustment of handicaps, which are within the jurisdiction of the National Unions concerned. See 1.08.

In order that players of differing competence may play together and be 'in competition', all amateur players are given a handicap at the outset. Where a player belongs to more than one Club, he must declare his 'Home Club', and report all 'away' results to that club for handicapping purposes. The highest handicap for men is 28, and for ladies 36. As a golfer improves, his handicap falls (and vice versa), with good to medium players having handicaps between 12 and 18, and very good players 11 or below.

Professional players do not have a handicap, and play off 'scratch' (in other words, zero).

Extremely good amateurs may reduce below zero until their handicaps are plus 1, plus 2, etc.

(a) Reducing your handicap

Handicaps are changed only when you play in what is called a 'medal' or 'qualifying' competition. All men's handicaps are divided into four categories, and for every stroke an individual's nett score is below the CSS (see 2.04), they are deducted either 0.1,0.2,0.3 or 0.4 of a stroke, as follows:

Player's Handicap	Category	Subtract for each stroke below par	Buffer zone
Up to 5	1	0.1	0 to +1
6 – 12	2	0.2	0 to +2
13 – 20	3	0.3	0 to +3
21 – 28	4	0.4	0 to +4

Consider the following four examples, one from each category, for 18 holes on a par 72 course with CSS 72.

Player	Gross score	Handicap*	Nett score	Score below par	Cat.	Deduction	New handicap
A	72	4.4 (4)	68	4	1	4 x 0.1 = 0.4	4.0 (4)
B	80	10.5 (11)	69	3	2	3 x 0.2 = 0.6	9.9 (10)
C	88	18.3 (18)	70	2	3	2 x 0.3 = 0.6	17.7 (18)
D	96	24.7 (25)	71	1	4	1 x 0.4 = 0.4	24.3 (24)

**See 2.06 for rounding up of handicaps to whole numbers (as in brackets above).*

You will see that Players A and C retained their handicaps, whilst Players B and D reduced theirs.

(b) Unchanging handicap

If your nett score equals the CSS (see 2.04), your handicap will remain unchanged. If your nett score is above the CSS but within the 'buffer' zone, it will also remain unchanged.

From the four examples above, each player could have scored as follows with no change being made to their handicaps:

Player	Nett score
A	72 to 73 inclusive
B	72 to 74 inclusive
C	72 to 75 inclusive
D	72 to 76 inclusive

(c) Increasing your handicap

If your nett score exceeds the CSS plus buffer zone, it will be increased by 0.1 only, no matter which category you are in, how large your score, or if you handed in a No Return (see 207).

If the four players above had scored the following, their handicaps would have increased as follows:

Player	Nett score	Adjustments
A	74 or above	4.4 + 0.1 = 4.5 (5)
B	75 or above	10.5 + 0.1 = 10.6 (11)
C	76 or above	18.3 + 0.1 = 18.4 (18)
D	77 or above	24.7 + 0.1 = 24.8 (25)

Note that they all increased by 0.1 only, but when

rounded up, Player A had his handicap increased by a full stroke, from 4 to 5. See 2.06.

For Ladies, handicapping was changed to the CONGU unified system on 1 February 2004. For competition purposes, a new category, 5, has been created, specifically for women with handicaps between 29 and 36. The maximum ladies' handicap of 36 ensures that nobody should ever have to give anyone more than two shots per hole.

Players must note that revisions to their handicaps apply immediately a medal or qualifying competition finishes (if two rounds are played, then after the second round). Therefore, if a player plays next day, at his own or another Club, any revised handicap will apply. Medal scores at 'away' Clubs must be declared. It is the practice of Clubs to display a list of all Members' handicaps and update it frequently. Computerised National Handicapping may well be introduced in the future.

For non-Club golfers, it is possible to obtain an 'Associate' handicap, officially recognised by the EGU and acceptable to affiliated Clubs (see 1.13).

2.06. Strokes received

Players will notice that calculations for handicap adjustments are made to the first decimal place, i.e. tenths of a stroke. However, strokes received in a competition are to the nearest whole number with the halfway point rounded upwards. For example:

Handicap	Strokes received
24.4	24
24.5	25
25.4	25
25.5	26

2.07. Strokeplay

Strokeplay consists of a player playing against the course. Any players playing with him are 'fellow competitors', rather than direct opponents. He plays 18 holes, calculates his total gross score, deducts the

strokes he receives (handicap) and determines his nett score for the round. This may be referred to as a qualifying or medal score. Example:-

Gross score = 100
Handicap = 24
Nett score = 76 *(four over par for a Par 72 course)*

His score of 76 may then be compared with the nett scores of fellow competitors to decide who is the champion or tournament winner.

The Club or Tournament Committee is responsible for the addition of scores and the application of the handicap recorded on the scorecard.

A competitor is responsible for the correctness of the score recorded for each hole on his card. If he signs his card for a score lower than actually taken, he shall be disqualified. If higher, the incorrect score stands.

Note that the 'strokes received' calculation takes place only once, at the completion of the round. Every stroke on every hole counts, whether it's a 1 or a 12! If you fail to score on any hole, or fail to complete the round, you must still hand in your card, marked 'NR' meaning 'No Return'. Your handicap will be increased by 0.1. See 2.04 and 2.05.

Do not practise beforehand on the course on the day of a strokeplay competition: you will be disqualified.

On occasion, a points system, e.g. Stableford, may be applied to a qualifying event, which would affect a player's handicap. The method of calculating Stableford points is shown in 2.08.

An 'Eclectic' is an individual strokeplay game over a specified number of rounds on the same course, whereby a player's best score at each hole is aggregated to give an 'eclectic' score for 18 holes.

2.08. Matchplay

Matchplay is where one or more players play in direct competition against one or more opponents. Results may be calculated either (1) on a hole-by-hole basis,

or (2) by the application of a points system. For either method, it is necessary to be familiar with the 'Stroke Index' of each hole. See 2.09.

For team events, the aggregate scores of individual matches will determine the winning team.

A player may practise on the course before a matchplay competition.

(1) Hole-by-hole

At each hole, a result is obtained for each player or partnership: win (+), loss (-) or draw (0).
Typical results over 18 holes could be:

- Player/Team A: 9; Player/Team B: 9
  = known as 'match halved'.
- Player/Team A: 10; Player/Team B: 8
  = Player/Team A wins, 'two up'.

Note that when a match has not been decided after 18 holes, the allocated handicap still applies for holes 19, 20, etc. See ROG Appendix I, part C, 11.

- Player/Team A: 10; Player/Team B: 6
  = Player/Team A wins, '4 and 2' (they are 4 holes up with 2 holes to play)

Note that individual matches may end before 18 holes have been completed. In this case, the players have completed 16 holes.

'Dormie' is the situation where only one side can win the individual match, but a halved match is possible if the losing side wins all of the remaining holes. For example: A 'dormie' 9-7 scoreline after 16 holes could result, after the next hole, in a 10-7 victory ('3 and 1') if the 17th is won by the player or team in the lead, or 9-8 (still 'dormie') if the trailing player or team wins the hole. In the event of a halved hole at 17, the leading side would remain two ahead but with only one hole to play, so they are declared the winners by '2 and 1'.

Similarly, 'dormie' 9-8 after 17 holes could result in a 10-8 win ('two up'), or a 9-9 tie (match halved).

Either way, the first-named side could only win or draw, and the second-named could only lose or draw. If the hole is halved, the leading side is still one hole up, but there are no holes left. They are therefore declared winners 'one-up'. Should the team trailing win the hole, the match will be 'halved', or shared. Once 'dormie,' the trailing side must win every hole remaining to halve the match.

'Dormie' applies only for a match of a stipulated number of holes. When a game, match or tournament has to conclude with a 'winner', decided if necessary by extra holes, then 'dormie' cannot apply.

(2) Points (Stableford)

Invented by Dr Frank Stableford, a Member of Wallasey and Royal Liverpool GCs in the 1930s, 'Stableford' is the most commonly used points system. The basis for scoring is shown on the table on the following page.

Strokes taken (par 3)	S'ford points	Strokes taken (par 4)	S'ford points	Strokes taken (par 5)	S'ford points
5+	Nil	6+	Nil	7+	Nil
4	1	5	1	6	1
3	2	4	2	5	2
2	3	3	3	4	3
1	4	2	4	3	4
-	-	1	5	2	5
-	-	-	-	1	6

As you can see, you receive two points for 3 strokes on a Par 3, for 4 on a Par 4 - or for 5 on a Par 5.

After you have applied the relevant handicapping calculations, you will note that a Stableford points total of 36 equates to a round played to par (35 points would be 1 over, 37 points would be 1 under, etc). Note that for holes where too many strokes are taken, Nil points are awarded (often referred to as a 'blob'). Players should not waste time putting-out on holes where they cannot score, but should move swiftly on.

Modifications of the Stableford points system include

Denver and Murphy, where points are deducted for scores over par but increased for scores below it.

2.09. Stroke Index

Every hole on a course is given a Stroke Index (S.I.) between 1 and 18. Lower numbers indicate a higher degree of difficulty than higher ones, but the indexing will also seek to provide a balance, and reflect how benefits should be distributed to players of differing capabilities when playing in competitions.

All stroke indices are shown on the scorecard of the course. Usually the men's S.I. will be different from the ladies' S.I. Where a player's handicap equals or is greater than the S.I. of a hole, that player receives one or more stroke(s). If it is lower, no stroke is received or other adjustment required.

(a) It follows that if a player has a handicap of 18, he will receive a shot on every hole, as his handicap will inevitably be equal to or greater than every S.I., since every hole will have an S.I. of 18 or fewer.

For example:

Hole	Par	Stroke Index	Gross Score	Nett Score	or S'ford Points
14	4	18	5	4	2

Note: In examples of calculations, I have shown two columns, one for Nett Score and one for Stableford Points. In practice, a scorecard will only have one column headed 'result', or similar.

(b) A player with a handicap of 12 would score as follows on the same hole:-

Hole	Par	Stroke Index	Gross Score	Nett Score	or Stableford Points
14	4	18	5	5	1

Note that in this example, the player's handicap is NOT equal to or greater than the S.I.

(c) A player with a handicap of 24 will receive two strokes on six holes – i.e. on those holes whose S.I. are 1, 2, 3, 4, 5, and 6 – and only one stroke on each of the holes with S.I.s 7 to 18 inclusive. A player with

a handicap of 25 will, similarly, receive two strokes on seven holes.

An example, for a 24-handicap player:

Hole	Par	Stroke Index	Gross Score	Nett Score	or Stableford Points
9	5	4	7	5	2

Note that the player's handicap of 24 equals or is greater than all 18 S.I.s once, and is greater than six of them a second time, here including hole 9, which has an S.I. of 4.

SCORING

2.10. A maths lesson

If you have read the preceding paragraphs, you are now able to check the adjustment of your handicap and understand the Stroke Index application. On the next page is a completed scorecard. Work through it to confirm the strokeplay nett score, and also the equivalent Stableford score. There is a deliberate mistake on one hole, although the column totals are correct. For answer see 5.04(a).

For a player with handicap of 14.
Quick tip - mark or tick each S.I. (1 to 14 in this example) before you start to play for easy reference once you're on the course.

Hole	Par	SI	Score	Res	S/F points	Hole	Par	SI	Score	Res	S/F points
1	4	5	4	3	3	10	4	11	5	4	2
2	4	8	5	4	2	11	4	14	6	6	-
3	5	3	4	3	4	12	3	18	4	4	1
4	3	17	4	4	1	13	4	13	5	4	2
5	4	9	6	5	1	14	3	16	4	4	1
6	4	7	4	3	3	15	4	12	4	3	3
7	3	15	4	4	1	16	5	2	6	5	2
8	5	1	4	3	4	17	4	10	4	3	3
9	4	6	3	2	4	18	5	4	4	3	4
OUT	36		38	31	23	IN	36		42	35	19
						OUT	36		38	31	23
						TOTAL	72		80	66	42

Notice that the total par of 72 happens to divide exactly – the par for each nine holes in this example is 36. The player's score of 38 on the front nine should be half the handicap (i.e. 7) different, i.e. 38–7=31, which it is. 'Minus' is used because the handicap is deducted from the gross score to give the nett result. This is also true of the back nine where 42–7=35.

With Stableford points, it is possible to cross-check, since for nine holes, par would be 9 x 2pts = 18. For the first nine holes, 23 pts is 5 pts better than par, i.e. 23 – 18 = 5. This checks with the fact that the nett result is five strokes less than par, i.e. 36 – 31 = 5. Similarly for the second nine, 19 Stableford points is 19 – 18 = 1 pt better than par, which is confirmed by 36 – 35 = 1 stroke. Overall totals also double-check, as 80 (gross score) – 14 (handicap) = 66 (nett score), 72 (par) – 66 (nett score) = 6, and 42 (back nine score) – 36 (back nine par) = 6.

Note that these cross-checks for Stableford do not apply if Nil points is recorded for one or more holes.

Given below is a scorecard without the calculations. Fill in the nett result and Stableford points columns for each hole, add them up, and find the totals for 18 holes. For answers see 5.04(b).

For a player with a handicap of 24.

Hole	Par	SI	Score	Res	S/F points	Hole	Par	SI	Score	Res	S/F points
1	4	11	5			10	5	2	6		
2	3	17	4			11	4	14	5		
3	4	5	4			12	3	16	5		
4	5	1	6			13	4	12	5		
5	4	13	4			14	5	4	7		
6	4	9	3			15	4	8	6		
7	5	3	7			16	4	10	6		
8	3	15	5			17	3	18	5		
9	4	7	4			18	4	6	2		
OUT	36					IN	36		5		
						OUT	36				
						TOTAL	72				

See Scoring Checklist at the end of SECTION 2.

Here is a scorecard with figures relating to the Championship tees. Do you know which famous course the figures refer to? See 5.04(c) for the answer.

Hole	Yards	Par	Hole	Yards	Par
1	376	4	10	379	4
2	413	4	11	174	3
3	397	4	12	314	4
4	464	4	13	430	4
5	568	5	14	581	5
6	412	4	15	456	4
7	388	4	16	424	4
8	175	3	17	455	4
9	352	4	18	357	4
OUT	3545	36	IN	3570	36
			OUT	3545	36
			TOTAL	7115	72

Note: Some scorecards have columns for white and yellow tees only with a separate card for Ladies' red tees. Others may have all three on the same card.

2.11. Teeing ground

Each hole has a teeing ground, from where you will play your first shot of the hole in question. Do not place your bag or trolley on the teeing ground, or on closely-mown adjacent areas which have been prepared for future teeing grounds. Find rougher ground nearby, and place your bag or trolley there.

On each tee you will find tee markers. White ones are for men's competitions and medals, Yellow for men's friendlies, Red for ladies (all events), and Blue for juniors. In addition there may be Professionals' tees behind the White tees.

These colours usually apply in the UK, but can be varied and may be different in other countries – you need to check. The positions of the tee markers may be changed on a daily basis by the greenkeepers. You must tee up your ball behind the two tee markers, but within the rectangular area defined by a line between the two tee markers and a maximum of two club

lengths behind them. You may place your feet outside this area if you wish.

A yardage and stroke index information board for each colour of tee may be placed on every tee. It shows the distances to the centre of the green from the permanent distance indicators on the tee, for each colour of tee marker on the tee. It will be necessary, therefore, to add or subtract the yardage between the indicator and the tee marker before playing. Scorecards will also show the yardages from the white, yellow and red permanent distance indicators.

In the UK, hole lengths are given in yards, whilst in many other countries they are in metres. To convert metres to yards, add 10% – e.g. 100m = 110 yards.

The order of play on the first tee is shown on the 'event' tee sheet, or more generally the lowest-handicapped player plays first, followed in ascending order of handicaps. The order of play can otherwise be determined by lot or ball chute.

For 'friendlies,' partners can be chosen by one player throwing a golf ball from each player into the air together and pairing the nearest two as they land.

Before teeing-off on the first tee, each player should announce the make of his ball. This ensures that when a ball is recovered after being feared lost, it is indeed the one that the player teed off with. Beware the players who carry a second ball in their pocket!

Divots on a teeing ground should not be replaced, as this would remove secure footing for those following. Frequently a container of divot mix (soil and grass seed) is provided for players to fill divots. Many courses in winter provide rubber mats or astroturf to avoid damage to the teeing grounds.

Ball-washers should be provided on all tees as it is essential to play with a clean ball whenever possible (see Glossary). Be aware that ball-washers may contain a detergent or an antifreeze.

2.12. Fairways

Fairways are the closely-mown areas of grass between the teeing ground and the green. The first player to play (the player with 'the honour'), is the one whose ball is farthest from the hole.

All divots should be retrieved, placed in the hole they came from and pressed down with the sole of a shoe.

All 'out-of bounds' boundaries will be marked with white stakes (see HOLES 3 and 10, SECTION 5).

Obstacles may include bunkers, trees, rocks, gorse, manhole covers and sprinkler heads – see HOLES 8, 9 and 10 in Section 4 for dealing with immovable/ movable obstructions and loose impediments, and HOLE 11 for a staked tree – or water hazards, which are shown by yellow or red stakes (see 2.15).

Most courses provide 'distance' markers along the fairways, which may take the form of a disc in the centre of the fairway or a painted pole at the side of the fairway (see Local Rules on reverse of scorecard for details). Usually, 'distance' markers are positioned 150 yards (137 metres) from the centre of the green. If you invest in a 'Rangefinder' instrument, remember to use it only for practice rounds.

2.13 Greens

Greens are the very closely-mown areas within which the holes are located. They may be surrounded by an area cut slightly longer, known as the fringe.

It is bad practice to take your trolley between a greenside bunker and the green itself. Always try to walk around the outside of the bunker.

Once your ball is on the green, or close enough for your next shot to be putted, be careful where you leave your bag. It is a sin to leave your equipment on the front apron of the green because, after putting-out, you will be walking towards the players behind and delaying their approach shots to the green. Before putting, draw a mental line between the flagstick on your green and the teeing ground of the next hole. Leave your bag or trolley along this line but, most importantly, not on the green, the fringe or the first cut.

Do not leave a dent on the green by leaning on your putter whilst waiting for others to play. The hole itself may be relocated anywhere on the green on a daily basis. Pitch marks, whether your own or any others you see, must be repaired.

Loose impediments, sand and loose soil, between the ball and the hole may be picked up or brushed aside. Marks made by shoe spikes may not be removed or flattened until all in your group have putted out. Do not hook the ball out of the hole using your putter head, as this may damage the hole.

A player must attempt to 'read' a green to find the line along which he should send his ball and the speed at which he should dispatch it (see 2.16, Putting).

Greens will be hollow-tined and top-dressed at specific times of the year – a small price to pay for well-tended and well-presented greens.

When you have putted out and replaced the flag, leave the green to those behind and take the shortest route to the next tee. The scores can be entered on the scorecard when you reach the next tee.

2.14. Bunkers

Bunkers are sand-filled obstacles, generally called 'traps' in the USA. On links courses - treeless courses next to the sea - bunkers can be 'pot' bunkers, which are deep and have steep revetted sides.

Other than greenside bunkers, bunkers should be located in the fairway and not in the rough.

Remember that your club must not be grounded – that is, touch the sand – before you make your stroke. (Extremely large areas of sandy wasteland on US courses are called 'waste areas', and in these your club may be grounded. In some places, for instance the Canary Islands, you will find 'picon', areas of crushed lava or volcanic dust usually treated as GUR (see Glossary).

In a bunker, you are not entitled to confirm that the ball which you have found is yours. Play the ball out – if it is not yours, ignore the strokes with the wrong ball and search again for your ball (see Glossary and Hole 4 in Section 4).

2.15. Water Hazards - Rule 26

There are two types of water hazard – firstly, those marked by yellow stakes, and secondly, those marked by red stakes and called 'lateral water hazards'.

(a) If your ball enters a water hazard with yellow stakes, you have three options:

- Play the ball as it lies.
- Play the ball from where you last played it.
- Drop the ball on a line from the flagstick to where your ball last crossed the margin of the hazard as marked by the yellow stakes with no limit to how far behind the water hazard the ball may be dropped.

(b) If your ball enters a lateral water hazard, marked with red stakes, then you also have a fourth option:

- Drop the ball within two club lengths of, and not nearer the hole, the point where the ball last crossed the margin of the hazard (as marked by the red stakes) or a point on the opposite margin of the hazard equidistant from the hole.

With the exception of playing the ball as it lies, all of the other options incur a one-stroke penalty.

Some water hazards may provide a dropping zone (see Competition or Local Rules). If a ball is 'lost' in a water hazard, the same options apply, except obviously "play the ball as it lies" (see Glossary). Also note that you cannot opt to play a 'provisional' ball if your original may be lost in a water hazard, unless there is a specific Local Rule (ROG Rule 26-1 applies).

2.16. Putting

Putting is known as the "game within a game". Whilst professionals hope not to exceed 30 putts per round, it is acknowledged that for an amateur, at least 50% of his total strokes may be on the putting green (by definition, on a par 4 hole). Due care and practice must therefore be given to this aspect of the game.

The types of grasses used on greens throughout the world vary widely and will affect your play. Of particular interest is the 'grain' of a green or, put more simply, in which direction is the grass pointing? Some will say that it always points downhill, some say it follows the direction of the sun. It will certainly follow the rollers of the mowing machines. Generally, if the grass is light green, the grain is away from you, and if it's dark green it's towards you. Be aware of the length of the grass – was it mown recently?

Greens normally rise up from the front to the back (although not always!), so that an approaching ball has a better chance of stopping. However, the slopes and gradients, humps and hollows all seek to make the 'reading' of a green a very skilful process.

Some say that greens always slope towards the nearest water, and you may wish to check this when deciding how much 'borrow' to take. 'Borrow' is the distance you will aim to one side of a hole in order for the ball to curve into the hole. Using a putter as a plumb-bob may or may not assist with this decision. Note that uphill putts take less borrow, while downhill putts exaggerate the borrow.

Note on putting terms: Latest developments include 'broomhandle' and 'belly' putters. A 'knee-trembler' is a three- to four-foot putt. If a putt does not 'drop', it may 'lip-out' or 'horseshoe'.

Etiquette is of particular importance on a green, because your behaviour will affect other players. Points to note are :-

- The ball farthest from the hole is the one to be played next, even if there are balls off the green that are nearer.
- If another is to play first, mark your ball (using a coin or something similar placed behind the ball… not at the side!) and pick the ball up.
- Do not walk on the line of another player's putt.
- Repair your pitchmark and any others you see.
- Remain quiet and still when another is playing.

- Start 'reading' your putt whilst others are playing – this saves time.
- Do not stand in another player's eyeline.
- Do not let your shadow cross the line of another player's putt, especially when attending the flagstick.
- Have the flagstick attended or removed when you are putting – it is not part of the course and you will incur a penalty if your ball strikes it as a result of a putt from on the green. You may decide it is prudent to have the flagstick attended by your partner, or removed altogether, rather than by your opponent! The reason is that if your opponent fails to remove the flagstick – maybe because it was stuck, or even because he wasn't paying attention – and your putt strikes it, your opponent may claim the hole. Strange but true!
- Leave the green promptly when all have putted so that players behind are not delayed.

When you have all putted out on the 18th green (or before, if a match has been decided) you should shake hands with the other players. This is a practice most enduring and endearing to the sport of golf.

SHOTS

2.17. Nine common golf shots

1. A straight shot, according to Jack Nicklaus, is the most difficult shot in golf. Here we have the swing, at impact, on a direct line to the target, with the clubface facing the target.
2. A draw is produced when the swing is straight but the clubface is 'closed' or pointing to the left of the target line. See 1.35, Grip.
3. A fade is achieved when the swing is straight but the clubface is 'open' or pointing to the right of the target line.
4. A pull is produced from an out-to-in swing at impact, but with the clubface square to the line of swing.
5. A duck, or quick, hook results from an out-to-in swing with a clubface 'closed' to the line of swing.
6. A slice is produced from an out-to-in swing with a clubface 'open' to the line of swing.
7. A push results from an in-to-out swing and a clubface that is 'square' to the line of swing at impact.
8. A hook is produced from an in-to-out swing and a clubface closed to the line of swing.
9. A quick slice results from an in-to-out swing and an open clubface.

To clarify or examine why certain shots behave in the way they do, it may be useful to consider this diagram

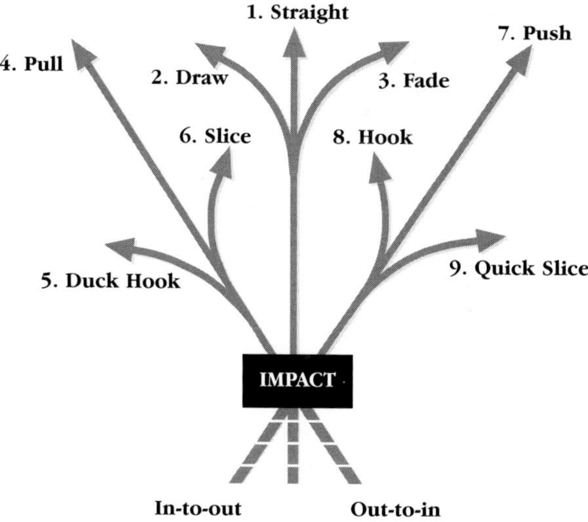

Shots 5 and 9 produce very little yardage, and the ball may never be seen again!

Shots 2 and 8 have the advantage of topspin, which will result in greater distance than 3 and 6. There is no guarantee that either will finish on the fairway.

If you can identify a trend in your shots, you can begin to analyse what you are doing and seek advice from the Professional.

Some, even professionals, accept and play to their non-straight shots. Colin Montgomerie, for example, has a natural fade as his stock shot. By aiming left of centre off the tee, therefore, he knows that his ball has a good chance of finishing on the fairway.

Note: You're playing 'out-to-in' when the club swings across the target line at impact from right to left as you face the hole. You're playing 'in-to-out' when the club swings across the target line at impact from left to right as you face the hole.

The clubface can be 'square ' – or at right-angles – either to the target line or the swing-path of the club. Equally, it is 'open' if it points to the right, or 'closed' if it points to the left of the swing-path.

A 'knock-down' shot is one where a low trajectory and no backspin is required. It is achieved using a longer club – one that can carry the ball further than

necessary – a closed clubface, (i.e. delofted, with the hands ahead of the clubface) and taking the ball back in the stance, (i.e. closer to the right heel) together with a shortened back-swing and follow through.

2.18. Shanks, Sclaffs, etc.

In addition to the nine common shots of golf dealt with in 2.17, there are many other 'unintended' shots in golf. Here are some of them (assuming, as always here, a right-handed player).

(a) The Shank. The ball flies off to the right, almost at right angles to the intended line. It does not go far. It is caused by hitting the ball half an inch from the heel of the club. Sometimes called a 'socket'.

(b) The Sclaff. The clubhead hits the ground behind the ball, often due to the player's incorrect transference of weight from left foot to right foot, instead of right foot to left foot, on the downswing. Usually called 'hitting it fat'.

(c) Skying. The ball rises quickly into the air, but does not go very far. The usual cause is that too much of the clubface is below the centre of the ball at impact.

(d) Topping. The ball sets off very low and is probably brought to a swift halt before reaching the fairway. It happens because too much of the clubface is above the centre of the ball, which is probably caused by the player lifting his head. Often referred to as 'hitting it thin', a 'grass cutter', or a 'worm burner'.

(e) Smothering. Here the problem is caused because the clubface, usually a wood, is hooded (i.e. 'closed' or delofted) at impact. Once again the ball will stay close to the ground.

2.19. Other forms of play

A player on his own may play a round and score, either as strokeplay or by Stableford points.

Two, as opponents, may play strokeplay, matchplay or score Stableford points. This is known as *'Singles'*.

Three may play *threesomes matchplay,* where one plays against two, with each side playing one ball (Rule 29). Or they may elect to play *threeball matchplay* (Rule 30), where all three play against each other, each playing his own ball, or *bestball* in which one plays against the better ball of two.

Variations of threeball include *on the perch*, where a point is awarded to each player for every hole won after the initial qualifying 'on the perch' hole. A player is 'knocked off the perch' when another wins a hole, but stays on if they halve it. The winner is the player with most points.

Another is *cricket*, which awards a maximum of six points per hole – either 4:2:0, 4:1:1, 3:3:0, or 2:2:2. Sometimes called barracuda.

Fourth man is an interesting game for three. An imaginary 'fourth man' plays to par on every hole, and partners each player in turn for six holes against the other two players, who act as partners. Which player takes the first six, middle six, and last six can be determined by rotation, handicap or mathematical apportionment of the stroke indices. The winner is the player with the most holes won during the six he 'played' with the fourth man – though if he loses a hole to a birdie, a hole is deducted from his tally. Each player plays to ¾ handicap.

Four players may play *foursomes matchplay*, in which two play against two and each side plays one ball, taking alternate shots (Rule 29). Sometimes, this format is varied, by allowing both partners on each team to drive on each tee and then selecting one ball only, with partners taking alternate shots to complete each hole – this is called '*greensomes*'.

Four players playing together is probably the most usual form of play. Normally the handicaps are based upon that of the lowest-handicapped player before the 3/4 matchplay reduction is applied. Example:-

Player	Handicap	Strokes received	Shot holes
A	13	NIL	NONE
B	15	2 [3/4x2 - see Stroke Allowance Table]	SI's 1 & 2
C	21	6 [3/4x8]	SI's 1 to 6
D	25	9 [3/4x12]	SI's 1 to 9

(See 2.09 to recall that your 'strokes received' [or adjusted handicap for the round] must be equal to, or greater than, the stroke index of the hole you are playing, to receive a shot.)

A really 'fun' game, involving much laughter, is *yellowsomes*, which is the same as greensomes, except that it's your opponents who tell you which of your drives you must take for your second shot at each hole. You, of course, tell them which of their balls you want them to play. It may take a long time!

Four players may also play *bestball matchplay*, where one plays against the best ball of three (Rule 30). More usual, however, is for four players to play *fourball matchplay*, in which two play their better ball against the better ball of the other two players.

In fourball strokeplay, two competitors play as partners, each playing his own ball. The lower score of the partners is the score for the hole (Rule 31).

Strokeplay competitions *Bogey*, *Par* and *Stableford*

are played against a fixed score at each hole (Rule 32).

When men and women play together in a competition it is called a '*Mixed*' match. A 'mixed foursomes' is sometimes called a 'mixed gruesomes'!

Texas Scramble (one eighth combined handicaps - strokeplay) is a form of play whereby a team of three or four all drive, choose the best drive and place their ball in turn at that spot, from which they then play their second shots. The process is then repeated until the first ball is holed, and a score recorded for that hole. Variants of the Texas Scramble include:

- *Drop Out Scramble* – the player whose ball is selected is not allowed to play the next shot.
- *Delaney Scramble* – the team mustn't choose more than two shots from any one player at each hole.
- *Ambrose Scramble* – the team must use at least four tee shots from each player.
- *Idaho Scramble* – the team must select the worst-placed ball each time.

American Foursomes involves a team of two, each driving on every hole. Each player then plays his second shot with his partner's ball. The better ball is now chosen and played alternatively as with foursomes (having discarded the non-selected ball.)

One; two; three (1;2;3) involves a team playing Stableford whereby one player's score (obviously the best score) is recorded for holes 1 to 6 inclusive. For holes 7 to 12, two players' scores are added and recorded, and for holes 13 to 18, three players' scores are added and recorded. A par score would be 72. Can also be played in reverse, as 3;2;1.

Confusion is a game where one point is awarded to the first player of the group to be on the green, one for the player who is closest to the hole and one for the first player to hole out.

Daytona (sometimes called Las Vegas) is for four players in two sides. The scores of a side for each hole are combined to form a number of points. If one player has a score of par or better, the lower score of the team is placed first. For example, if the scores on a par 3 are 3 and 4, then the team's score is 34. But, if the best score for the hole is over par, then the higher must be placed first. For example, if the scores on a par 3 are 4 and 5, then the team score is 54. The side with the lower number of points is the winner.

Full House is a game in which a player is set a points target calculated by deducting his handicap from 36. The winner is the player who exceeds his target by the most points. Scoring is 8 points for an eagle, 4 for a birdie, 2 for par and 1 for bogey.

Flag Competition is a strokeplay game in which each player has a small flag or similar marker. When a player has played the number of strokes equal to the par for the course plus his handicap, he places the marker on the course at that point. The winner is the player who goes furthest along the course with his allotted strokes – this usually involves playing the first few holes twice.

Example: gross score = 89 after 18 holes. Deduct 20 handicap = nett score 69, or three under par if the course has a par of 72. The player therefore has three extra shots up the first hole, his nineteenth. This, too, has a counter-check system – gross score 89 +

extra shots 3 = 92 = par 72 + handicap 20.

A *Limited Club* competition can be played under any format, requiring only that each player is restricted in the number of clubs he can use for the round. The usual 14 clubs could be reduced, for example, to a putter and three others of the player's choice.

A *Skins* game is one in which scoring is by holes won. If a hole is not won outright by one player, the next counts as two, or if money per hole is involved, the money rolls forward until it is won.

Sixes is a matchplay game for two sides of two. Each player plays six holes as partner with each of the other three players. For each six holes, the winners receive 2 points each, or all four receive 1 point each if the six-hole match is halved.

Medalford is played individually with full handicap, the front nine holes as a Medal and the back nine as a Stableford. Gross score is recorded on first nine and totalled. Deduct half handicap allowance - rounded up - to record nett score.

The second nine holes are recorded with gross score, and allowances according to the stroke index, as for a Stableford. Points should be recorded. To complete the card, the Stableford points from the second nine should be deducted from the first nine nett score.

For example (with 20 handicap): Front nine gross = 50, minus half handicap = 40 nett. Back nine = 20 Stableford points. Result = 40 – 20 = 20.

Yellow Ball is played with a team of four. The yellow ball is allocated to each team member in turn, the lowest handicapper first. The player with the yellow ball earns points for the team's total. The team with the most points wins. If the yellow ball is lost, the team stops scoring. If no team completes 18 holes, the team with the most points wins, or if tied, the team which completed most holes wins. A variant involves adding the best score from the other players at each hole to the yellow-ball score at that hole.

Medal-Matchplay May be singles or 4-ball-better-ball. Each hole results in a score against par for each side. The actual scores are carried forward on every hole.

Both sides must hole out on every hole, as in medalplay. The winners are the side with the better final score against par.

Bisque is matchplay against the course in two, three or fourballs. Full handicaps apply, but the strokes of each player are used wherever that player decides, i.e. wherever he needs them most – but not more than one at any hole. Each player announces at the completion of each hole whether he wants to use one of his shots or not. If a player beats nett par he marks +, for a par score he marks 0, and if he's above nett par, –. Scores are determined by deducting minuses from pluses for the round.

The Snake. If a player has three putts on a green, he receives 'the snake'. It passes to the next player who three-putts, but now it is doubled. The person who holds 'the snake' at the end of the round has to pay up, or buy the drinks, to the value of the snake eg. x2, x3, x4,etc. The pressure on putting is enormous!!

Dovetail. A strokeplay game for pairs. Each player must contribute a score for nine of the 18 holes. At the end of each hole, the pair must decide which player's score should be counted. Consternation reigns as the pair realise that they may have chosen badly as the end of the round approaches!

PS. 'Nearest the Flag' is a common feature, but for me, 'Nearest the Fairway' is a favourite!

2.20. Stroke Allowances

When competitors play in a medal, i.e. strokeplay, their full handicap is applied. However, in other forms of play, allowances less than full handicaps may generally be employed.

Singles matchplay. The lower handicap is subtracted from the higher handicap and the difference is multiplied by 3/4. eg. 24 – 16 = 8 x 3/4 = 6. This means that the better player of the two has to give 6 strokes to his opponent (at holes with stroke indices of 1, 2, 3, 4, 5, and 6).

[Remember the Golden Rule – an (adjusted)

handicap must be equal to or greater than the stroke index of the hole in question, for a player to receive a stroke.]

Greensomes matchplay. Here the combined handicap of the partners is determined from a Greensome Handicap Table – marked by * below – and the difference between the two pairs of opponents is multiplied by 3/4. The resultant number is the number of strokes given. Example:

first pair 28 + 32 = 30 *

second pair 16 + 20 =18 *

Difference = 12 x 3/4 = 9 strokes given to the first pair.

So the better pair give their opponents shots on half the holes during the round – those holes with an S.I. of 9 or fewer (see inside back cover).

Singles Stableford. As for Singles matchplay above, but the difference is multiplied by 7/8. (Full allowance can be applied). So strokes are given by the better players at holes with a stroke index of 7 or less.

Foursomes matchplay and *Greensomes Stableford*. As for Greensomes matchplay above, but the difference is multiplied by 3/8. Example:

first pair 22 + 26 = 48

second pair 14 + 18 = 32

Difference = 16 x 3/8 = 6 strokes given to first pair

So strokes are given by the better pair at holes with stroke index of 6 or less.

Foursomes Stableford. As for Greensomes matchplay, but the difference is multiplied by 7/16. Example:

first pair 22 + 26 = 48

second pair 14 + 18 = 32

Difference = 16 x 7/16 = 7 strokes given to first pair

So strokes are given to the better pair at holes with a stroke index of 7 or less.

Strokeplay. For foursomes medalplay the allowance is normally 1/2.

For 3-ball or 4-ball, medal or Stableford, the allowance is normally 3/4.

Competitions. Entrants in a competition have the stroke allowances applied to their own handicaps only, e.g. a pair in a Greensome Stableford might be:

(13 + 22)/2 = 17 handicap * from the Greensome Handicap Table. Multiply by 3/8 of the combined handicap from the Stroke Allowances table.

Note Where a lady receives 'courtesy strokes' (in a 'mixed' team), then these strokes are added to the combined pair's allowance. Example:

22 + 26 = 48 x 7/16 = 21 plus 3 courtesy strokes = 24 stroke allowance for the pair.

Note When combined handicaps result in a half (eg 18 + 21 = 39 39/2 = 19.5) then for medalplay the exact half applies, but for Stableford the figure is rounded up to the next whole figure (in this case 20).

Stroke allowances are recommended by CONGU to the Golf Unions and to the Ladies Golf Union. However, each Union may vary the actual allowances and so variations from those given in the Stroke Allowances table will occur. Application of handicaps and allowances will also depend upon whether the event in question is a 'non-qualifier' or a medal competition.

The Stroke Allowances table gives generally recommended Stroke Allowances (see inside back cover).

2.21. Entering competitions

Clubs hold various competitions throughout the year, which are normally listed in advance on an annual programme. Some are for men only, some for ladies only, and some are mixed. There are also Juniors, Seniors and Veterans events, and knockout competitions are held, for which the finals are contested in the late summer.

Competitions, either serious or friendly, may also be held against other Clubs, other Counties, etc.

Usually competition entries and fees are dealt with in the Professional's shop.

2.22. 'Two's' competitions

When entering a competition, it is often possible also to enter a 'two's' competition. This ensures that should you score a 2 on a hole, or even on two or more holes, you will receive a proportion of the entry monies. Mostly, even if you have a terrible score in a medal competition, it is still worth trying for a 2.

When a 2 is scored you, and your marker, should circle the number '2' where entered on the scorecards to alert the competition organisers.

2.23. Playing restrictions

If you join a Club, it is important that you establish any restrictions upon when you may play. There are usually days set aside for men only and for ladies only. There may also be days set aside for seniors, veterans, juniors and societies.

Attempting to play on the 'wrong' day or at the

'wrong' time may well lead to acute embarrassment – you have been warned!

2.24. Slow play

Slow play is a constant source of annoyance. Golf has a certain speed and rhythm, and when this is interrupted, partners, opponents and other players can become very impatient. The proper course of action is for the slower group to 'invite' the group behind to go past them. This is called 'letting them through' and should always happen if the slower group fall a hole behind the group in front of them.

Note that a player has only five minutes to look for a lost ball: if in doubt let the following group through.

Two-ball matches should have precedence over, and be entitled to pass, any three- or four-ball matches, who should 'invite them through'. A single player has no standing, and should give way to a group of any kind. A group playing a competition match should always be let through at the earliest opportunity. Check your course rules on precedence.

Slow play will be avoided if players:

- are ready to play their own shots on the tees and fairways
- always play a 'provisional' ball if their ball may be lost
- wave the next group through if searching for a lost ball
- line up their putts when approaching and on the greens
- only enter the scores on the cards when they reach the next tee.

IT IS NOT GOOD ENOUGH TO KEEP AHEAD OF THE GROUP BEHIND, YOU MUST KEEP UP WITH THE GROUP AHEAD!

The threepart checklist on the next page may be helpful.

A. BEFORE YOU START

- Obtain a scorecard from the Pro's shop.
- Check type of play – i.e. strokeplay or matchplay?
- Check event type ie. Friendly? Fourball? Greensome? Mixed? Etc.?
- Check partner(s) handicap(s) and the allocation of strokes received, e.g. full handicap? 3/4 handicap? 1/2 combined? 3/8 combined? Or other?
- Check you have a usable pencil or biro! Do not erase mistakes. Cross out, agree correct with marker and initial.
- On your scorecard write your name, your partner's name, event title, date, start time, handicap(s) and strokes received.
- Exchange cards with your opponent(s).

B. DURING PLAY

- Fill in your opponent's score in the main column of his/their card.
- Fill in your own (or combined) score in the column marked 'Markers Score' (normally on the left hand side of the card.)

C. UPON COMPLETION OF PLAY

- Make sure that the score entered for each hole, for you and your opponents, is correct by comparing cards.
- When satisfied, sign your opponent's card as Marker, and hand it to him/them.
- When satisfied, sign your own card as Player, and hand it to the event's organiser as directed.

FAILURE TO COMPLETE THE FINAL TWO STEPS ABOVE WILL RESULT IN DISQUALIFICATION!

ALWAYS MAKE SURE, BY DOUBLE CHECKING, THAT YOU HAVE YOUR MARKER'S SIGNATURE ON YOUR OWN CARD, AND THAT YOU HAVE SIGNED IT YOURSELF BEFORE HANDING IT IN.

Note: you may have calculated Stableford points as you played each hole and arrived at a total upon completion. You may wish to total your strokes in strokeplay, deduct your 'strokes received' and obtain a nett score, but you are not signing your card for these calculations, which are the responsibility of the event organisers or Committee. You may wish to do so on most occasions, and certainly for 'friendlies' – how otherwise do you know who is going to buy the drinks?

Calculations for any handicap changes will be based upon your actual scores, the Standard Scratch Score (SSS) and the Competition Standard Scratch (CSS).

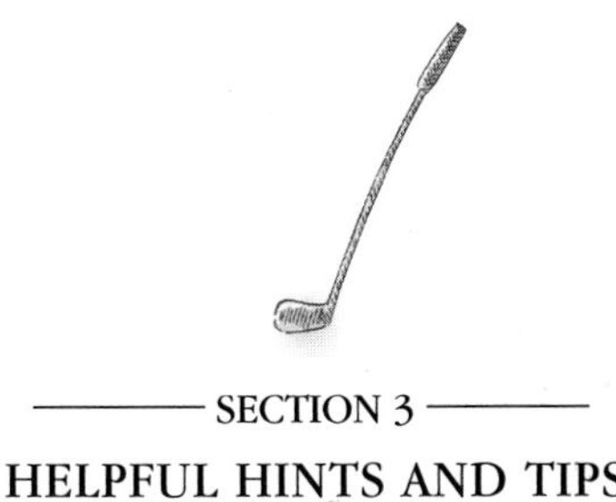

SECTION 3
HELPFUL HINTS AND TIPS

Taking lessons; course management; keeping calm; knowing the Rules.

3.00. Lessons

- Learn how to play golf by taking lessons with a PGA Professional. This section is intended as an aide-memoire, not a lesson in itself. The better you play, the more you will want to play better.

3.01. On the Tee

- Always check wind direction and speed.
- Ask yourself "Where do I want my ball to be in relation to bunkers and my next shot into the green?" 'Course Management' applies anywhere on the course. Always think about the shot you have to make after the next one. Visualise your shot. Remember that sometimes two 7-irons are better than a driver and a wedge. Tiger Woods is said to 'plan' each hole from green to tee.
- A player who normally slices would usually play from the right-hand side of the teeing ground, and vice-versa for one who normally hooks.
- If using a wood off the tee, tee up the ball so that its 'equator' is level with the top of the

clubhead when grounded.

- Do not be embarrassed to use a 3-wood off the tee. A 3-wood has increased loft, which gives it greater backspin and therefore longer 'carry'. The shot will also be straighter. Some players never use a driver (1-wood).
- Align your clubhead behind the ball before placing your feet in position. When you have grounded your club and placed your feet in position for the shot (stance), you are 'addressing' the ball.
- For all golf shots, look at the back of the ball whilst striking.
- If you accidentally knock the ball off the tee peg before making a stroke at it, (or it falls off of its own accord), no stroke is counted (despite the chorus around you of "one!"), and you may replace it.
- Use divot mix if provided.
- Do not stand in another player's eyeline whilst they are taking their stance and making a stroke anywhere on the course. Either stand behind them (i.e. looking at their back) or in front of them (i.e. looking at the top of their head).

3.02. On the Fairway

- For an elevated green, take more club than the distance requires, eg. a 7-iron instead of an 8-iron.
- For a green a long way below you, take less club than the distance requires, eg. a pitching wedge instead of a 9-iron.
- To practice chipping, try hitting balls under a bench, from about six feet away, with a sand wedge – keep the ball back in the stance and your hands ahead of the ball. You may be pleasantly surprised by the result!
- To pitch-and-run, take a 7- or 8-iron and play it as a putt. Land the ball halfway to the hole in winter and one-third of the way in summer. Do not bend the wrists.
- Always make sure you have a clean clubface and grooves before making your stroke.
- To help with club selection, find which club gets you to the green from the 150 yards marker, then add or subtract approximately 10 yards for each club nearer or farther from the green your ball is positioned. Thus, if you reach the green from 150 yards with a 6-iron, a shot of 140 yards will

require a 7-iron, and one of 130 yards an 8-iron; conversely, a 160-yard shot demands a 5-iron, and a 170-yarder a 4-iron, and so on.

3.03. In the Rough

- Always check that the ball is yours. (see Glossary)
- Grip the club very firmly.
- Drop the clubhead very steeply down onto the back of the ball.

3.04. In a Bunker

- Decide whether to play forwards, sideways or backwards. A few extra yards from the fairway is preferable to another bunker shot.
- Do not touch loose impediments, e.g. leaves, twigs, divots, or anything natural – even banana skins!
- You may remove stones only if your course has a Local Rule to permit this – see reverse of the scorecard the club provides.

- Moveable obstructions that are man-made may be removed, e.g. drinks cans and the like.
- Do not touch the sand with your club prior to making your stroke.
- Open stance and clubface, take a full swing and follow through.
- Strike the sand about 2 inches behind the ball – more for a short shot to a nearby flag, less for a longer shot.
- Use a pitching wedge in wet sand (rather than your sand wedge).
- Always rake the bunker before leaving. Some courses prefer that rakes be left in bunkers, others outside. Find out which, and comply.
- Strive never to play out of one hazard and into another.

3.05. In the Water

- You are allowed to play a moving ball in water.
- Do not touch the water with your clubhead before making your stroke.
- If you are playing your ball from inside a yellow or

red line (or stakes), do not touch the ground with your clubhead prior to making your stroke.

3.06. In the Trees

- If your ball is against the right-hand side of a tree as you face the green, try playing left-handed with the back of the clubhead or with the clubhead pointing downwards. Alternatively, try facing backwards and swinging through with the right arm only. This applies in reverse for a left-handed player on the other side of a tree.
- Try a forced shot to keep below branches, e.g. a 3-iron with the ball back in the stance and a shortened follow-through.

3.07. On the Green

- Always consider other players.
- If just off the green, remember that a poor putt is usually better than a good chip!
- Shots from off the green may hit a ball already on

the green with no penalty, but the 'moved' ball must be replaced to its original position and the 'offending' ball played as it lies.

- Repair your pitchmark and any others you see. Do not repair spike marks on your line of putt.
- You may brush aside sand and loose soil on your line of putt, but do not press anything down.
- Look at the line of your intended putt whilst waiting for others to play. Will it move left or right? Is it uphill or downhill? Do not lean on your putter; it could leave an indentation on the green.
- Check the grain of the grass, which may follow the sun or the mower rollers – if the grass is light green, the grain will be away from you and the putt will move faster, whereas dark green grass indicates that the grain is towards you and the putt will travel more slowly…or perhaps it means the grain is across the ball's path! Greens will, as a generalisation, slope towards nearby water.
- Watch other players' putts to gain knowledge of slopes and borrows.
- You may find it helpful to place the ball with the manufacturer's name along the line you wish to putt – this is called 'logo-lining'.

- Have a procedure or pre-shot routine and stick to it without wasting time.
- Keep your head still – do not follow the ball with your eyes. Listen to a short putt drop before looking up. "Left shoulder up - in the cup."
- If your ball rolls past the hole when playing long putts, watch its movements closely – this will help you with the putt back.
- Remember in matchplay that if you are putting for a 'half', there is no point in hitting a soft putt that trickles off-line. If you miss, you do not have another stroke because you will already have lost the hole – so be positive!
- Note that if your opponent in a match attends the flagstick with your authority, but fails to remove it and your ball strikes it, you lose the hole even if the putt goes in! Perhaps best to ask your partner to attend rather than your opponent, or have the flag removed in the first place.
- If you have a dodgy back, why not remove your ball from the hole using a rubber sucker attached to the handle of your putter?
- If you have to move your marker one clubhead to the side to let another player putt, do something

different to remind you to replace it – e.g. put your ball in the opposite pocket to normal.

- Always ask another player to mark and pick up his ball if there is any chance of your putt hitting his ball. The onus is on you to ask. In strokeplay, if your putt does strike another ball on the putting green, there is a penalty to you of two strokes (Rule 19-5(a)), and the other player's ball must be replaced in its original position. No penalty in match play.

3.08. In the cold and wet

- Take extra towels and spare gloves.
- Take large winter gloves or handwarmers.
- Keep grips dry.
- Wear waterproof trousers to keep trouser legs dry and free from mud.
- Be aware that golf balls travel less far in cold air and on wet greens.
- Always clean your ball when the rules allow (e.g.

on the tees and greens, with preferred lies, abnormal ground conditions, embedded ball, etc).

3.09. Uphill

- Ball nearer left heel.
- Take more club, e.g a 3-iron instead of a 4-iron.
- Keep shoulders parallel to the slope.

3.10. Downhill

- Ball nearer right heel.
- Take less club, e.g a 6-iron instead of a 5-iron.
- Keep shoulders parallel to slope.

3.11. Ball on slope below feet

- Ball will tend to slice, so aim a little left with clubface slightly closed.
- Keep posture but extend arms.

3.12. Ball on slope above feet

- Ball will tend to hook, so aim a little to the right with clubface slightly open.
- Keep posture but place hands lower on the grip (known as 'choking down').

3.13. In the wind

- Check wind direction and speed.
- "In the breeze – swing with ease."
- Do not try to hit the ball harder.
- Try to keep it low into the wind by having the ball farther back in your stance, and fly it high if the wind is behind you.

3.14. Golf bag

- With a carry-bag, use a tripod to keep it, and you, dry.
- Double shoulder straps help to avoid back strain.
- If you are carrying, you may wish to take fewer

clubs (leave the umbrella behind as well if weather is suitable – it's quite heavy).

3.15. Travelling abroad

- Pack your clubs head-first in your bag for better protection.
- Obtain a large travelling bag to contain your golf bag, clubs, shoes, waterproofs, etc.
- Don't forget to take sun hat, sunglasses, sunscreen, insect repellent, anti-histamine cream and, most importantly, your handicap certificate.
- On course, drink plenty of water before you feel the need (even if the sun is not shining!)

3.16. Rhythm

- The rhythm or tempo of a golf swing is a measure of the 'fluency' of the backswing and the downswing. The 'swing' should be one continuous movement with no sharp jerks. Maximum acceleration should be at the point of impact. One way of practising good tempo is to swing a club with your feet together. Having mastered this, try a full backswing and follow-through whilst standing on your left leg only – but you must retain your balance throughout. Be gentle – don't sprain any muscles by being over-enthusiastic.

3.17. Temperament

- Try to remain cool, calm and collected. There is no doubt that verbal abuse, temper tantrums and the like will cause a player to become tense and spoil his game, and very likely that of his playing companions. Gentlemanly conduct should be the order of the day on a golf course - you'll play better, too! As Des Lynam said when he tried to have golf consigned to TV's Room 101, "it exacts a terrible revenge for every bit of pleasure you get from it". If you're having problems, you're not the only one!

3.18. Rules

- Obtain your free copy of the RULES OF GOLF. Read, mark, learn and inwardly digest.

3.19. Enjoy

"*Don't worry, don't hurry. We are only here a little time, so never forget to stop and smell the flowers.*" Walter Hagen.

SECTION FOUR

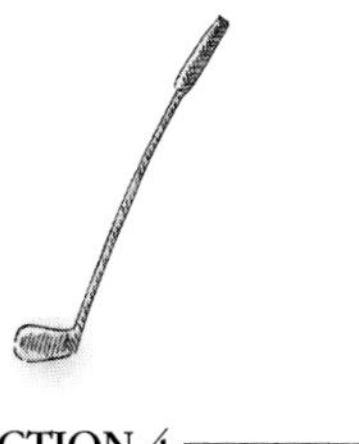

SECTION 4

A TESTING ROUND OF GOLF

...complete with the slings and arrows of outrageous golfing fortune!

Note:- You'll find a 'Quick reference' list after HOLE 18, pointing to the problems and Rules encountered.

HOLE 1

Player A meets Player B on the first tee and they discuss whether to play:-

either *(i) Medal Play* – all strokes to be recorded at every hole. At the completion of the round, total strokes minus handicaps give nett scores to decide the winner (lower total).

or *(ii) Stableford points* – the strokes for each hole to be recorded. During, or at the completion of, the round, handicaps should be applied to each hole and, depending upon the Stroke Index, the number of points determined. The higher points total decides the winner.

or *(iii) Matchplay* – each hole to be won, halved or lost with a running score kept so that each player knows by how many holes he is leading or trailing. Handicaps to be applied at each hole depending

upon stroke index. The winner is the player who wins most holes, which may be before the completion of 18 holes, or the match may be halved. Having decided the form of play, it is agreed that Player A will tee off first as he has the lower handicap.

Both players declare their make of ball and their identification mark on the ball, and wish each other "Play Well".

HOLE 2

Player B drives into the deep rough. He decides that his ball may be difficult to find and announces to his opponent that he will "play a provisional". *(Note: this is very wise because if he cannot find his original tee shot he would have to walk all the way back to the tee to play another ball.)*

The players go forward and start to search for Player B's ball. They have 5 minutes to search from when the search starts. The ball is found and Player B plays his second shot. The provisional ball is picked up. *(Note: if the original ball had not been found, Player B would, after 5 minutes, play his fourth shot with the provisional ball – i.e. first tee shot, plus penalty and provisional tee shot, then fourth shot. For definition of 'lost ball', see ROG.)*

HOLE 3

Player A strikes his second shot over white stakes alongside the course boundary. These indicate "out of bounds". He has, therefore, under penalty of one stroke, to drop a ball as near as possible to where the original was last played, and play his fourth shot – i.e. tee shot + second shot out of bounds + plus penalty = three shots before playing the dropped ball. *(Note: it is considered bad course design to locate white stakes within the boundaries of a course.)*

HOLE 4

Player B plays his ball into a bunker and finds it covered by sand. He may remove by probing, raking or other means as much thereof as will enable him to see a part of a ball. If an excess is removed, no penalty is incurred, and the ball shall be re-covered so that only a part of the ball is visible. If the ball is moved it shall be replaced, and, if necessary, be covered. Player B is careful not to touch the sand with his clubhead before making his stroke. *(Note: at this point Player B is not entitled to know if the ball he has found is his or not. He must play the ball from the bunker and, if he then finds it is his, play on. If it is not his, he must search again and repeat the process. No strokes are counted for playing a ball which was not his in a bunker.)*

HOLE 5

Player A plays his second shot into a lake. The lake is bordered by yellow stakes indicating a water hazard. He may choose:-

(i) to play the ball as it lies, making sure not to touch the water with his clubhead prior to his stroke.

(ii) under penalty of one stroke, play a ball as near as possible to the spot from which the original ball was last played.

(iii) under penalty of one stroke, drop a ball behind the water hazard, keeping the point at which the original ball last crossed the margin of the water hazard, (i.e. the line between the yellow stakes) directly between the flagstick and the spot on which the ball is to be dropped, with no limit to how far behind the water hazard the ball may be dropped.

HOLE 6

Player B plays a poor tee shot towards a stream and an out-of-bounds fence which runs alongside the fairway. Although he sensibly has played a 'provisional' ball in case the ball is out of bounds, upon arrival at the stream, his ball is clearly visible in two feet of water. This ball is therefore the ball 'in play', and he must abandon his 'provisional' ball.

The stream is bounded by red stakes - a 'lateral water hazard'. This means that the option to choose to go back on a line *(see HOLE 5 (iii))* may not be possible, as the player's ball would still be in the stream.

Therefore, in addition to the choices (i), (ii) and (iii) given for a water hazard *(see Hole 5)*, a fourth option is now available:-

(iv) under penalty of one stroke, drop a ball outside the water hazard within two club lengths of - and not nearer the hole than - a point where the original ball last crossed the margin of the lateral water hazard (i.e. the line between the red stakes) or, if necessary, a point on the opposite margin of the lateral water hazard equidistant from the hole.

HOLE 7

Player A plays a very high shot which lands in a wet area of the fairway. Upon inspection he finds that the ball is embedded in its own pitchmark. He retrieves the ball, cleans it, and drops it without penalty as near as possible to the spot where it lay but not nearer the hole. *(Note: Player A must not repair the pitchmark on his 'line of play' until after he has completed his next stroke – this is only permitted for a pitchmark on a green, i.e. 'line of putt'. Also, in extremely wet situations, a Club may make a Local Rule that permits dropping an embedded ball in the rough, but not in sand.)*

Upon reaching the green, Player B requests Player A

to "attend the flag". Once the putt has been struck, Player A must remove the flagstick before the ball reaches the hole. *(Note: the flagstick does not form part of the course, or of the game. It is an indicator of the hole position only.)*

A flagstick in the hole may be struck by a ball played from off the green but otherwise penalties are involved. A flagstick may be removed before a ball is struck from either off the green or on the green. If a ball rests against the flagstick when it is in the hole, the player may move, or remove, the flagstick, and if the ball falls into the hole he is deemed to have holed out with his last stroke.

HOLE 8

Player B plays his second shot, which comes to rest on an iron drainage cover. This is classed as an 'obstruction' because it is 'artificial', in other words 'man-made'. It would be impossible to move it because of its size or weight.

Player B therefore has an 'immovable obstruction' from which he may obtain free relief. The cover is 'through the green', which means it is not on a teeing ground or putting green or in a hazard. Without penalty, therefore, Player B lifts his ball, cleans it and drops it within one clublength of - and not nearer the hole than - the nearest point of relief. *(Note: Relief is available when a ball is in or on an obstruction, or the obstruction interferes with the player's stance or swing.)*

(Further note: If the drainage cover had been in a bunker, the ball must be dropped in the bunker. If the cover had been on a putting green, the ball may be placed. There is no relief without penalty if the ball is in a water hazard, or lateral water hazard.)

HOLE 9

Player A plays his ball, which comes to rest just in front of a yellow stake defining a water hazard. The ball is not in the hazard, but the stake is on his line of play and would interfere with his stance or swing. The stake is an 'obstruction', because it is 'artificial', or 'man-made'. It is easily moved (and replaced after the shot), and therefore is a 'movable obstruction', from which Player A may obtain free relief. He removes the stake, plays his shot and replaces the stake. *(Note: Free relief may also be obtained from red stakes denoting a lateral water hazard, and other lightweight, artificial objects. However, white stakes denoting 'out of bounds' are not movable obstructions – they are deemed to be fixed, and if the ball is in bounds, it must be played as it lies.)*

HOLE 10

Player B plays his second shot, which hits a tree, falls to the ground, and comes to rest under a fallen branch. The branch is an 'impediment', rather than an 'obstruction', because it is not 'man-made' but is natural – such as stones, leaves and twigs. Because it is movable, it is a 'loose impediment', and may therefore be moved without disturbing the ball and placed to one side without penalty. Player B now plays his shot to the green. *(Note: Loose impediments in a bunker may not be moved, and the ball must be played as it lies even if covered by twigs or leaves. Check scorecard for a Local Rule, which may allow you to remove stones in bunkers.)*

Meanwhile, Player A has played a long, hooking second shot, and finds his ball touching the line between white stakes denoting 'out of bounds'. Player A knows that objects defining out of bounds, such as walls, fences, stakes, railings and lines, are

themselves out of bounds, the actual line being determined by the inside points at ground level. He also knows that a ball is out of bounds only when all of it is. His ball is touching the inside of the line, but is not over it - he therefore gratefully plays to the green. *(Note: Player A is permitted to stand outside the 'out of bounds' line to play his shot. As indicated in HOLE 9, however, he may not remove a white stake to improve his stance or swing.)*

HOLE 11

Player B's tee shot comes to rest next to the trunk of a staked tree, which would impede his backswing. In making a practice backswing, he is very careful not to remove any leaves from the tree, as this would invoke a penalty. He finds the 'nearest point of relief' - not the one he might prefer, but the one in closest proximity. For a right-hander, this will probably be to the left of the tree when facing the green, as point of relief to the right of the tree would have to allow for the distance from ball to feet, plus feet to top of backswing, which must, of course, be clear of the tree.

Player B marks the point, and drops the ball within one club length of the point - and not nearer the hole - without penalty. *(Note: if the ball when dropped had rolled nearer the hole or rolled more than two club lengths from where it struck the ground, it would have to have been redropped. If the error was repeated again, the ball may be placed at the point it struck the ground on the re-drop. Further note: Check your scorecard for Local Rules concerning the protection of young trees. Usually, plastic sheaths have the same meaning as stakes).*

Player A's ball has come to rest in a gorse bush and he declares it 'unplayable'. His options are:-

a) play at the spot from which the ball was originally played.

b) drop a ball within two club lengths of the spot where the ball lies in the bush (not from the nearest point of relief).

c) drop a ball behind the point where the ball lay, keeping that point between the flagstick and where the ball is dropped, as far back as he chooses.

Player A drops on a line back, and accepts a penalty shot, which is applicable to all three options.

(Note: A player may declare his ball 'unplayable' anywhere on the course except in a water hazard. If in a bunker, a), b) and c) above apply, but the ball must be dropped in the bunker.)

HOLE 12

Player B finds that his ball has come to rest in an area

of 'casual water', defined as temporary accumulation of water not in a water hazard. Snow and natural ice are counted as casual water or as loose impediments. Dew and frost are not casual water. Player B makes a footprint which fills with water – his opponent agrees 'casual water'. Player B marks the nearest point of relief and drops the ball within one club length - and not nearer the hole - without penalty, and plays his next shot. *(Note: ruling also applies if the casual water is in a bunker or on a green. On a green it is placed at the nearest point of relief.)*

Players A and B have been making good progress, but the group in front have lost at least one hole on the players in front of them. A & B are therefore invited to 'play through'. This normally happens at a teeing ground, but may happen anywhere on the course.

(Note: All players are urged to keep up with the group ahead and not just ahead of the players following. In the absence of Special Rules, a group of 3 or 4 players should let a group of 2 players 'play through,' especially if matches are being played.)

HOLE 13

Player A's second shot rolls into an area surrounded by stakes and/or lines, with a small sign stuck in the middle of it which says 'GUR'. This stands for 'Ground Under Repair'. Player A knows that, although it is not mandatory to take relief (unless there is a Local Rule) the greenkeepers wish to keep players off this area so he determines the 'nearest' point of relief, which is not necessarily the point he would have preferred, and not nearer the hole. He drops within one club length, without penalty. *(Note: This ruling applies if the GUR is in a bunker or on a green. On a green the ball is placed at the nearest point of relief.)*

HOLE 14

Both players are on the green, but Player B's ball is directly on the line of Player A's putt to the hole.

Player A asks Player B to mark his ball, which he does by placing a small coin behind the ball. He then lifts the ball, thus taking it 'out of play'.

However, Player A does not want his ball to strike the coin, so he asks Player B to kindly move it to one side. Player B willingly does this, placing the toe of his putter against the coin, lining up the putter head with a nearby landmark, and then moving the coin to the heel of the putter head.

Player A can now putt to the hole, after which Player B must remember to reverse the process by placing the heel of the putter against the coin, lining up the putter head with the same tree, and placing the coin at the toe. He now places the ball in front of the coin, which he picks up. He plays his putt.

(Note: Player B took his ball out of play when he originally marked it with the coin. He was thereafter entitled to move the coin as described. It would have been quite wrong, and subject to penalty, if he had placed his putter head against the ball and moved the ball one club head length sideways, as this would have been interfering with a ball in play.)

HOLE 15

In walking back to the 15th tee, Player A decides to leave his trolley at the side of the fairway. Unfortunately, he plays a low slice off the tee, and his ball hits his trolley before bouncing on to the fairway. Player A knows that his trolley is part of his 'equipment', i.e. anything used, worn or carried by himself (except his ball in play and coins or tee pegs), and therefore his penalty is loss of hole (matchplay), or two strokes added (stroke/medal play). This also applies if a ball rebounds and hits the player himself. *(Note: If his ball had struck his opponent's equipment, no penalty would be incurred. If a ball in motion is accidentally deflected or stopped by an outside agency, such as a green keeper's tractor, it is considered 'rub of the green', no penalty is incurred, and the ball shall be played as it lies. If a ball in play and at rest is moved by another ball in motion after a stroke, then the 'moved' ball must be replaced.)*

HOLE 16

Player B is in a bunker. He tries to scoop the ball out, but in so doing his clubhead strikes the ball more than once. Player B must count the original stroke and add a penalty stroke, making two strokes in all.

Meanwhile, Player A's tee shot, his best of the day, bounded 200 yards down the fairway and stopped near some bushes. To his amazement, a fox runs across the fairway, picks up the ball in its mouth and disappears into the bushes. Player A walks forward to the spot where the ball was last seen at rest, but there is no sign of it, so he declares the fox to be an 'outside agency', drops a replacement ball at the spot, and plays his next shot to the green without penalty. *(Note: the fox may have been any other thief - even one of the human variety!)*

HOLE 17

Both players strike their tee shots into deep rough in the same area, 30 yards to the left of the fairway. They both start to search, Player A finds a ball and decides to play it. He then goes to help Player B find his ball. Player B finds his own ball and another ball which he knows from the identification mark belongs to Player A. Player A accepts that he has played a 'wrong ball', and that the penalty is loss of hole (matchplay), or two strokes added (stroke/medal play). He plays the correct ball (stroke number 4), and abandons the one he originally hit from the rough. *(Note: If either Player had hit a 'wrong ball' from a bunker, there would be no penalty* (see HOLE 4)*)*.

HOLE 18

The Clubhouse is now in sight. The final fairway is lined with conifers, and Player B manages to hit his second shot, a high slice, into the trees and out of view. Although he could play a 'provisional' in case he cannot find his ball, he confidently decides that the ball will have fallen to the ground under a tree.

He is correct, but the ball is in a rabbit scrape. He tells Player A that he wishes to take relief from the scrape, but Player A has to be satisfied that Player B would have been able to play from the spot where the ball lay under the tree, even if there had not been a scrape.

He is satisfied, so Player B measures one club length from the edge of the scrape, (i.e. the nearest point of relief) and drops the ball within it, without penalty. He is very fortunate because, although the ball strikes the ground within the club length, the slope of the

ground away from the trees enables the ball to roll another club length onto the fairway! Player A accepts Player B's good fortune, as the ball came to rest within two club lengths of where it first struck the ground, but not nearer the hole, and therefore did not have to be re-dropped.

(Note: The above situation frequently occurs on tree-lined courses. The nub of the argument is that if the Player whose ball is under the tree could not have played a stroke at the ball because of trees, fences, walls etc., he cannot escape by using the rabbit scrape as a ruling.)

Having putted out on the eighteenth green, the two players remove their caps, shake hands, and exchange pleasantries such as "well played" or "I enjoyed the game".

In the bar afterwards, one is heard saying "we were both playing nicely, when on the 16th this fox appears..."

Quick reference

1 FORM OF PLAY/ORDER OF PLAY/BALL IDENTIFICATION
2 PROVISIONAL BALL/5 MINUTES SEARCH
3 OUT OF BOUNDS (See also HOLE 10)
4 BALL IN BUNKER
5 WATER HAZARD
6 LATERAL WATER HAZARD
7 EMBEDDED BALL/ATTENDING FLAGSTICK
8 IMMOVABLE OBSTRUCTION
9 MOVABLE OBSTRUCTION
10 LOOSE IMPEDIMENT/WHITE STAKES (See also HOLE 3)
11 STAKED TREE/UNPLAYABLE BALL
12 CASUAL WATER/ PLAYING THROUGH
13 GROUND UNDER REPAIR (GUR)
14 MARKING BALL POSITION
15 EQUIPMENT
16 DOUBLE HIT/OUTSIDE AGENCY
17 WRONG BALL
18 BURROWING ANIMAL/DROPPING BALL

SECTION 5

A STUDY OF THE MOST FREQUENTLY-USED RULES OF GOLF

"If in doubt, play the course as you find it and play the ball as it lies."

"And if you can't do either, do what is fair. But to do what is fair, you need to know the Rules of Golf."

Extracts from the ROG.

5.00. Breakdown of the Rules

We probably use 20% of the Rules, 80% of the time – so here is a list of those most frequently encountered. The sections and subsections refer to the RULES OF GOLF.

Section I. Etiquette.

Section II. Definitions.

Section III. The Rules of Play.

1-3 You may not agree to waive the Rules.

2-4 Gimmies

3-5 General penalties - matchplay = loss of hole - strokeplay = two strokes *(See 5.02 for one-stroke situations)*

4-4 Maximum 14 clubs

6-3 Start time

6-5 Mark your ball for identification

6-6 Sign cards upon completion of play

6-7 Slow play

7 Practice before or between rounds

8-2 Line of play

10 Order of play

11 Teeing ground

12 Search for and identify ball

13 Ball played as it lies

13-2 Back-swing - do not improve

13-4 Do not touch sand or water with club

14-4 Double hit *(add 1 penalty shot)*

14-5 Playing a moving ball

15-3 Wrong ball

16-1 Line of putt

17 Flagstick

18 Ball at rest moved

19 Ball in motion deflected or stopped

20-1 Lifting and marking

20-2 Dropping and redropping

23 Loose impediments

24-1 Movable obstruction

24-2 Immovable obstruction *(See 5.01 (1))*

25 Abnormal Ground Conditions (casual water, GUR, hole made by burrowing animal *(See 5.01 (1))*

25-2 Embedded ball

26 Water hazards *(See 5.01 (2))*

27-2 Provisional ball

28 Ball unplayable *(See 5.01 (2))*

Note: As a general rule, when you have a 'free' (without penalty) drop, you must drop the ball within one club length of the nearest point of relief (eg GUR).

However, when you have a 'penalty' drop (perhaps to add one stroke to your score), then you may drop the ball within two club lengths of the nearest point of relief.

5.01. Examples of 'Relief' situations

(1) Without penalty/one club length

24-2 Immovable obstruction (also includes ' staked' trees - see Local Rule on reverse of scorecard)

25-1 Abnormal Ground Conditions

25-3 Wrong putting green

(2) With penalty/two club lengths

26-1c Lateral water hazard

28 Ball unplayable

5.02. Examples of 'one stroke only' penalties

As a general rule, penalties are loss of hole (matchplay), the addition of two strokes to your score (strokeplay), or disqualification.

There are, however, many situations where only a one-stroke penalty applies...

5-3;12-2;18. Lifting your ball without announcing your intention and/or marking it and/or inviting your opponent to observe what you are doing - you should do all three!

6-7 Slow play - note penalties.

6-8c Failure to mark and report at discontinuance of play.

14-4 Double hit.

16-2 Ball overhanging hole.

18 Ball at rest moved.

20 Incorrect dropping or placing.

21 Cleaning ball (during play of hole).

25-1b Dropping ball outside bunker.

26-1; 26-2. Ball in water hazard.

27 'Stroke and distance' applies to 'lost' ball, 'out of bounds' and the playing of a 'non-provisional' ball.

28 Ball unplayable.

5.03. Tips on the Rules

(1) You need to know that:-
may = optional
should = recommendation
must = instruction (and penalty if not carried out)
a ball = you may substitute another ball
the ball = you may not substitute another ball

(2) Many of the rules are listed under 'Ball' in the ROG.

(3) When a rules problem occurs which may have to be decided by the Club Secretary or others, often after the round has been completed, make sure that you can tell him the form of play; who was involved; where the incident occurred; and in some cases the player's intentions and any subsequent events.

(4) Frequently players seek relief from a rabbit scrape when their ball lies in a difficult spot, perhaps under a tree. The player should ask his opponent to confirm that the rabbit scrape is genuine and, more importantly, that he would have a possible shot if the rabbit scrape had not been there. If he might have had such a shot, and the scrape (or other burrowing animal scrape) is genuine, then he can have a 'free' drop within one club length of the nearest point of relief *(See Section 5 - HOLE 18)*. If there is no possible shot, then he must either play it as it lies or declare it 'unplayable', and under penalty of one stroke, drop it within two club-lengths.

(5) You will see in the HOLE 18 situation that a 'dropped' ball may roll outside the prescribed club length so long as it does not roll further than two club lengths from where it struck the ground, or nearer the hole *(See Rule 20-2c(vi))*. This means that the ball may now be nearly three club lengths from the original nearest point of relief.

(In the case of a two club lengths ruling

(penalty for 'unplayable' ball and so on), then it can finish nearly four club lengths from the original position – but not nearer the hole.) This all depends on the slope of the ground, of course, and may act in the opposite direction to that which the player may have wished – or indeed it may not act at all. Some you win, some you lose!

(6) Further to (5) above, always remember that you must not touch or lift a ball 'in play' until you have marked its position with a tee peg. When measuring club lengths, remove the clubhead cover first, place a tee peg at each end of the club, and remove the club before you drop the ball.

(7) If you want to be able to quote at least one Rule by heart, then let it be 24-2b, which refers to relief from an immovable obstruction and occurs regularly (including 'staked' trees under Local Rules). Your friends will be most impressed – unless they also have a copy of this book!

5.04 Answers from 2.10

[a] Correct scorecard:-

Hole	Par	SI	Score	Result	S/F pts	Hole	Par	SI	Score	Result	S/F pts
1	4	5	4	3	3	10	4	11	5	4	2
2	4	8	5	4	2	11	4	14	6	5	1
3	5	3	4	3	4	12	3	18	4	4	1
4	3	17	4	4	1	13	4	13	5	4	2
5	4	9	6	5	1	14	3	16	4	4	1
6	4	7	4	3	3	15	4	12	4	3	3
7	3	15	4	4	1	16	5	2	6	5	2
8	5	1	4	3	4	17	4	10	4	3	3
9	4	6	3	2	4	18	5	4	4	3	4
OUT	36		38	31	23	IN	36		42	35	19
						OUT	36		38	31	23
						TOTAL	72		80	66	42

Hole 11 should be corrected as above.

[b] Completed scorecard should be as below:-

Hole	Par	SI	Score	Result	S/F pts	Hole	Par	SI	Score	Result	S/F pts
1	4	11	5	4	2	10	5	2	6	4	3
2	3	17	4	3	2	11	4	14	5	4	2
3	4	5	4	2	4	12	3	16	5	4	1
4	5	1	6	4	3	13	4	12	5	4	2
5	4	13	4	3	3	14	5	4	7	5	2
6	4	9	3	2	4	15	4	8	6	5	1
7	5	3	7	5	2	16	4	10	5	4	2
8	3	15	5	4	1	17	3	18	2	1	4
9	4	7	4	3	3	18	4	6	5	3	3
OUT	36		42	30	24	IN	36		46	34	20
						OUT	36		42	30	24
						TOTAL	72		88	64	44

Did you have the correct answers?

[c] Mystery scorecard?

The yardages and pars are those presented to the contestants for the 2000 Open on the Old Course at St. Andrews.

SECTION FIVE

GLOSSARY

SECTION 6

GLOSSARY

Some of the terms and expressions you might hear when you're on the course… or in the 19th hole. And some of the reasoning behind the unique language.

19th Hole

Another name for the clubhouse bar…

Abnormal Ground Conditions *(see Rule 25)*

These are areas of casual water (see HOLE 12, Section 4), ground under repair (see HOLE 13) or holes made by burrowing animals (see HOLE 18).

Accelerate

For any stroke you make in golf with any club, the clubhead must be accelerating when it strikes the ball. Failure to do this will inevitably result in a bad shot.

Ace

A hole in one. (Usually on a par 3, unusually on a par 4!) The successful player is expected to buy a drink in the 19th hole for all those present when he has finished his round. You can insure against this.

A number of opportunities exist to record your hole in one and receive a prize – perhaps a special tie or a bottle of whisky.

Most players never score an ace in the whole of their playing lives, whilst for some strange reason once a golfer has had a hole in one, very often he will go on to achieve a number of others. Golf statistics show many interesting facts about those who have achieved this prestigious feat.

Address

To 'address' the ball requires that (except in a hazard) two actions are taken:-

(a) your feet are placed ready to make your stroke – this is called your 'stance';

and (b) your club is grounded – i.e. the clubhead rests on the ground behind the ball.

Once both of these actions have taken place, you are penalised one stroke if the ball moves before you start to strike it, and the ball must be replaced in its original position. You must therefore be very careful in windy conditions.

In a hazard, you are not permitted to touch the sand, or the water, with the clubhead. You have therefore addressed the ball when you have taken your stance.

Do not forget that hazards are usually marked by a line on the ground, and if you intend to play the ball as it lies within the hazard, although your ball may not be in sand or water, you must not ground your club.

Advice

In a competition, a player must not ask for, or give, 'advice' from or to another player which could influence a player in determining his play, e.g. "What club did you use?"

He may however give 'information' which is public knowledge, such as the position of hazards or the application of the Rules.

Air shot

When it is the clear intention of a player to strike his ball, but the clubhead fails to make any contact, this is called an 'air' shot. It must be recorded as a stroke, but there is no additional penalty. The player may continue with another stroke, unless playing foursomes, in which case it is now his partner's turn to play the ball as it lies.

Albatross

When a golfer takes three shots fewer than par at a hole – i.e. a 2 at a par 5 – it is known as an albatross. Many golfers never see one, except in a Monty Python sketch. Called a double eagle in the USA.

Alligators

If playing in the USA, you may find a red line surrounding a wooded area. This indicates that it is unsafe to enter the wooded area because of the possible presence of alligators (or snakes). It is foolish therefore to search for a lost ball beyond the red line! See scorecard for Local Rules and warnings.

Apron

The apron is the mown area of fairway immediately approaching and joined to the green. It is the area upon which a well-struck ball should land, bounce, and roll onto the green.

Artisan

In days gone by, even the Professional at a Club was not allowed to enter the Clubhouse, which was for Members only. For tradesmen and craftsmen who wanted to play golf, but for whatever reason could not become Members of a Club, a separate section was formed in many Clubs, whereby 'Artisans' – as they were called – could have a separate clubhouse somewhere on the course, and play at certain specified times. Although many of the old traditions have long since disappeared, there are still Artisans attached to many Clubs even today.

Back nine

The final nine holes played in an 18-hole round.

Backspin

Backspin is imparted to a golf ball by the angle between the vertical and the clubhead face. This angle varies from about 5 1/2 degrees for a wood to roughly 64 degrees for a lob wedge. The backspin is encouraged by the friction between the ball and the clubface surface, provided in part by grooves. The shape and dimensions of these grooves are carefully specified by the R & A.

Players are advised to keep their clubface grooves well cleaned. Backspin is severely curtailed if there is grass between the ball and the clubface, e.g. when playing from the rough. It may result in a 'flier'.

For medium- and short-iron shots to the green, backspin is strongly imparted by hitting 'down' on the ball and taking a divot. This seeks to 'control' the ball, which will still have backspin when it lands on the green. Professionals strive to land the ball just short of the hole – it will then bounce forward past the hole, but on its second bounce the backspin will cause it to back up towards the hole.

It will be appreciated that the 'control' exercised by Professionals avoids the problem encountered by medium- and high-handicapped amateurs, for whom a ball without backspin usually bounces through the green.

Baffie

The old name for a 4-wood.

Ball

Pernicious, spherical, dimpled object which refuses to go where you want it to.

lost …

A ball is deemed lost if not found within five minutes of beginning to search for it (this does not include the time taken to arrive at the anticipated location of the ball). It is also deemed lost if another ball is put into play, or a 'provisional' ball is played nearer the hole than where the ball is thought to be (or may subsequently be found to be). For a ball lost in a

water hazard, see 2.15 and Rule 26-1.

Apocryphal stories abound of some courses, which reputedly have signs indicating that "golf balls are not deemed to be lost until they have stopped rolling"!

marking position of … in play.

The position of a ball may be marked, and the ball lifted, anywhere on the course, subject to the Rules. Except on the green, and at other specified times – see Drop Zone, below – the ball must not be cleaned (Rule 22). On the green, the position of all the balls, except the one being putted, should be marked by placing a ball marker, or small coin, immediately behind each ball (not at the side!) before it is lifted (Rule 20-1). If a marker interferes with the play, stance or stroke of another player, it should be moved one or more clubhead-lengths to one side. Note that it is the marker-to-marker measurement which is made, not a distance from a ball. A ball must be marked first, and removed from play before the marker is moved sideways.

Once a ball has been replaced on the green, it is 'in play', even if the marker has not been picked up. If the ball then moves, perhaps due to the wind, it shall be played from where it comes to rest. If it has rolled into a hazard, the appropriate rules apply.

…personalising

It is every golfer's responsibility to be able to identify his own ball (Rule 5). This is done before play by using a marker pen or stamping machine to make a personal mark. Make sure you take enough personalised golf balls with you.

On the course, a ball's identity may not be immediately obvious. A player is entitled to lift it to find out if it is his (Rule 12-2).

Before doing so, however, he must do three things :-

- annouce his intention to his opponent or fellow competitor
- mark the position of the ball, perhaps with a tee peg
- give his opponent or fellow competitor an opportunity to observe the lifting and replacement.

Failure to do any one of these three actions will incur a penalty stroke. The player may only clean the ball to the extent necessary to identify it.

In a hazard - sand or water - the procedure is different (Rule 12-1 applies). If a ball is covered by sand or loose impediments in a bunker, the player may probe or rake, enabling him to see part of a ball. It may not be his ball, but at this point he must re-cover it with sand or loose impediments, so that only part of it is visible. The ball must then be played – hopefully out of the bunker. If it is his own ball, the player plays on. If, however, it is not his ball, then it must be abandoned, with strokes counted. The procedure to find his own ball in the sand is repeated. The same procedure applies in a water hazard - if the ball is moved, it is replaced with no penalty (proceed under Rule 26-1).

provisional...

A 'provisional' ball is one which is played from the same place as one which may be lost (outside a water hazard) or may be out of bounds. When employed, it can save a great deal of time, and also an embarrassing walk back to where the original ball was last played. The player must inform his opponent or fellow competitor that he "intends to play a provisional." If he's still on the tee, he shall play it after others on the tee have played their tee shots, but before moving forward.

If he fails to inform accordingly, the second ball he strikes is the ball in play under penalty of one stroke – i.e., if the original ball was off the tee, he is now regarded as playing his THIRD shot off the tee, and his original ball if found must be abandoned. If the original ball is found (having declared a 'provisional'), the 'provisional 'ball must be abandoned, and no strokes are counted for the 'provisional' ball.

Note that the player must make his decision before moving forward. He cannot play two shots, i.e. the original plus a second 'provisional' ball, and then decide what to do when he reaches one or both balls. If no "This is a provisional" statement is made, the second ball, with penalty, is the ball 'in play', even if the original is found in an excellent position.

If a player does not declare a 'provisional', but then fails to find his tee shot, he is permitted to tee up his next ball when he returns to the tee.

seconds …

A ball which has been used, e.g. one that may be found on the course, becomes a 'second'.

x-out …

If during manufacture a ball is found to be imperfect, it is stamped with crosses and called an 'x-out'. An x-out must not be used in a competition.

Ball chute

A ball chute is a piece of open metal pipe mounted on a stand and placed near the 1st tee. Its purpose is to determine the order in which players shall play if a tee sheet is not in operation. Upon arrival at the course, a player places a ball in the chute behind any others already there. When his ball is the next one out, he and his partners may drive from the first tee after the group ahead.

Bandit

A 'bandit' is a golfer whose handicap appears to be too high for his golfing abilty – as decided by his golfing opponents!

Betting

Betting on the results or outcome of professional tournaments is universal, and odds are frequently displayed on T.V. Personal bets between amateur players on the result of their own games vary from significant amounts of money to who has to buy the drinks in the bar afterwards. Golfers generally seem to like an incentive to play well. There may be an extra 10p for birdies, for instance, or arrangements made on sandies (or 'sand-save') and brandies (or 'golden ferret') – these refer to holing out in, respectively, two shots or one shot from a bunker – or ouzalems (on a Par 3 in 1, nearest the pin, down in 3).

A Nassau is a scoring system favoured by high-betting players. One point is allocated to the winner of the front nine, another to the winner of the back nine and a third to the winner of the full eighteen holes. Cash may be substituted for points!

Birdie

When a golfer takes one shot fewer than par at a hole – e.g. a 2 at a par 3 – it is known as a birdie. One theory as to why birds' names are used in golf terminology is that some early American golfers were playing and one of them scored one under par. His partner exclaimed "My, that was some bird!" Afterwards 'birdie' became the accepted description of this score and was naturally applied in like terms to other scores.

Blading

Trying to dislodge a ball caught in fringe grass at the edge of a green may result in the iron clubhead becoming 'snagged', resulting in a poor shot. One way of dealing with this is to take a wedge and hit the 'equator' of the ball with the leading edge of the clubface – this is called 'blading' or using a 'belly-wedge'. Another way is to use, for example, a 3-wood to putt the ball. This also avoids snagging, but both shots require much practice.

Blind hole

One at which you may play a shot without being able to see the green towards which you are playing. Usually, a direction post indicates your line of play.

Brassie

The old name for a 2-wood.

Bogey

When a golfer takes one shot more than par at a hole – e.g. a 5 at a par 4 – it is known as a bogey. It is also quite common to take double bogeys, triple bogeys, and so on, but it's better not to think about it.

Call hole

On some holes, for safety and speed-of-play reasons, players will be advised to mark their golf balls (very often on the green of a par 3), and stand aside to allow the players behind to play their next shots (very often their tee shots on a par 3). The first group then

continues as usual. Players may often find a bell, or other noisy device, on a blind fairway, which should be rung to advise the players behind that it is now safe to play their next shots.

Carry

Carry is the length in distance, or the time in seconds – sometimes called 'hang time' – that a ball remains in the air between being struck and landing for its first bounce.

Carry is extremely important to the player who has to propel his ball over intervening hazards such as bunkers or water. Ideally, a player should know the 'carry' distance for each of his clubs.

Cleek

The old name for a chipping iron.

Countback

In the event that two or more players have the same nett score, having taken into account the respective handicaps for holes 10 to 18, the winner may be determined by the better back 9, back 6, back 3 or back 1. What this means is that the player with the better nett score for the last nine holes (10 to 18) would be declared the winner.

If the nett scores are the same for the last nine holes, the nett scores for the last six holes (13 to 18) are examined. If these are the same then the last 3 holes (16 – 18) are checked. If there is still not an outright winner, the last hole may be the decider, failing which the front nine holes may be examined in the same way. Joint-winners could be declared unless the competition specifies a play-off or the toss of a coin. This is also known as a (score)card play-off.

Cup

The hole on the green is referred to as the 'cup'. It is 4 1/4 inches in diameter. A ball has been 'holed' when it is at rest within the circumference of the hole, and all of it is below the level of the lip of the hole.

Cut

Most professional tournaments on Tour consist of four rounds, played over four days. Generally approximately 156 players play in threes, based on a draw for partners, which remains the same for the first two days. Each day, the order of play of each group is completely reversed.

After two days (two rounds) the 'cut' is made, reducing the number of players to approximately 78 and ties, though in some tournaments, those players within 10 shots of the leader qualify. Those who miss the 'cut' leave with no prize money. The remainder play the final two days (two rounds) in pairs, with the highest-scoring players starting first each day, and the

lowest-scoring (or leading) players last. Prize money is distributed according to final scores, having declared a Tournament Champion.

Dimples

If a golf ball had a smooth surface with no dimples, its trajectory would be the same as that of a thrown stone (i.e. a parabola), because its highest point in the air would be halfway between the thrower and the point where it lands. It would also not travel very far.

Dimples are indentations which – apart from reducing drag by creating turbulence – provide a similar effect to the aileron shape of an aeroplane's wings. Air is trapped in each dimple, and as the ball in flight has backspin, the air pockets on top of the ball have a higher velocity than those underneath the ball. The increased velocity reduces the pressure and causes a 'lifting' effect on the top of the ball, whilst underneath the reduced velocity increases the pressure and causes an upward 'pushing' effect. As long as it has significant backspin, therefore, a ball will strive to stay in the air longer and travel a greater distance. Once the backspin stops, the 'lifting' effects are lost and the ball plummets from the sky.

Dimples, which were introduced in 1905, have a very important part to play in the design of a golf ball. Their shape and number will vary according to the manufacturer, and will include such descriptions as octahedron, duodecahedron and many others. The number of dimples on a ball may well exceed 400. Launch angle, trajectory, hang time and many other issues are all part of the high-technology design of modern-day golf balls.

As an aside, a football is made using 32 panels, of which 20 are hexagons and 12 are pentagons – a combination which creates the simplest spherical solid…the truncated icosahedron!

Disc Golf

A game originating in America, involving throwing specially-designed flying discs at baskets. The course comprises 9 or 18 different targets, and scoring is similar to traditional golf. Anyone interested?

Divots

A word derived from the old Scots, originally meaning squares of turf used as roofing material.

Divots are the lumps of soil and grass thrown up by the golf club when making a stroke. Professionals are very prone to 'taking' divots, because they seek to strike the ball before the turf, thus imparting backspin. It is essential that divots are collected by the player, or his caddie, and replaced into the hole from which they came before tamping down with applied pressure from a shoe. Failure to do this is very much frowned upon, as not only does it leave the course littered with clods of earth and grass, but a bare patch remains, which will take a long time to grow over.

When your ball next lands in an unrepaired divot, you will 'bless' the player who left it unattended!

Some courses provide divot repair pegs, which are biodegradable and intended to hold divots in place during regrowth.

Dog-leg

This is a hole at which the fairway bends or kinks, either to the left (right-to-left dog-leg) or to the right (left-to-right dog-leg). Normally, it is the objective of a player to place his drive near the corner or 'elbow' of the dogleg, so that there is a clear second (or third or fourth!) shot to the green.

Drive-in

At Member Golf Clubs, a new Captain is elected every year. At the start of their year in office, it is traditional that they 'drive-in', which requires that the newly-installed Captain tees up on the first tee and drives a ball, hopefully down the first fairway.

Often a prize is given to the person who predicts the closest point to where the ball will finish. Knowledge of the new Captain's game is therefore an advantage – even if an insult is not intended!

Dropping

When a ball has to be dropped, or redropped, in accordance with the RULES OF GOLF, a player must stand upright facing in any direction, holding the ball in his hand, with his arm extended straight out and at shoulder height. He shall then drop the ball by releasing it, without trying to influence it in any way.

When playing foursomes, it is the 'next partner to play' who must drop the ball when required.

Drop Zone

Drop zones are often provided when artificial immovable obstructions, for example spectator stands (called 'bleachers' in the USA), prevent the normal application of the rules. The zones are indicated by a white line, enclosing an area into which the ball is to be dropped with no penalty.

Duff

A 'duff', 'muff' or 'fluff' is a failed shot, one which usually travels a short distance, always to the acute embarrassment of the player!

Eagle

When a golfer takes two shots fewer than par at a hole – e.g. a 2 at a par 4 – it is known as an eagle. Eagle sightings are not quite as rare as that of the albatross.

Equity

If a situation arises which is not covered by the RULES OF GOLF (and there cannot be many!), a decision is made which is fair to the player(s) involved. This is called 'in equity'.

First Cut (and Second Cut)

Around the greens and along each side of the fairways, you may find strips where the grass is longer than on the greens or fairways but shorter than the rough – perhaps 1 to 1 1/2 inches long. These strips are called the 'first cut', and provide a transition between the closely-mown areas of the fairway and the longer rough. You must not apply 'Winter Rules' (Preferred Lies) on them, as they are not fairway. There may also be a 'second cut' of slightly longer grass.

Flagstick

The flagstick, often referred to as the 'pin', does not form part of the game and is provided only as an indicator of where the hole is positioned on the green on any particular day. A ball struck from off the green may strike the flagstick with no penalty, but a ball struck on the green must not touch the flagstick, and is subject to penalty if it does so. It should therefore be removed before the stroke is made or held, and be 'attended' by another player, who must remove it after the ball has been struck but before it reaches the hole (see 2.16). It is good practice for the player attending the flagstick to stop the actual flag from flapping in the wind whilst his partner is putting.

Where a green has two tiers, a course will often

indicate which tier the hole has been placed on, by placing a basket or second flag on the flagstick. Frequently the colour of the flags will change between the front 9 (which may be red) and the back 9 (yellow).

Flop shot

This is a shot played with a very lofted club (perhaps a lob wedge or sand wedge) from off the green. It is intended to climb steeply, land softly and stop quickly.

'Fore'

As golf was developing many years ago, it was common practice for players to have not only a caddie, but also a fore caddie. This person would be positioned along the fairway to see where his player's ball finished. Having struck the ball, the player would call "Forecaddie!" to alert the forecaddie to the fact that he had played his ball. This call became abbreviated over time to "Fore", and although 'ball-spotters' are often used nowadays, the cry must be made by the player who sees his ball flying towards someone on the course. Golf is a dangerous game, and to be struck by a golf ball can be traumatic.

Therefore, always call "Fore" if there is any chance that your ball might strike someone – this at least gives those in the line of flight a chance to protect themselves or take evasive action.

If in doubt – SHOUT!

There is nobody as sorry as the player who did not shout "Fore" and his ball injured someone. You have been warned!

Front nine

The first nine holes played in a round on an 18-hole course.

Gamesmanship

Frowned upon by most but practised by some, attempts by a player to seek advantage over his opponent by devious or doubtful means – or gamesmanship – can be employed in golf as in any sport. Matchplay is the most fruitful area in golf where there may be opportunities to practise upsetting your opponent(s).

Gap wedge

Some manufacturers adjust the loft of their irons to give greater distance compared with rival's equipment. This may happen through the range, including the pitching wedge, but not the sand iron. You will see, therefore, that a 'gap', or increase, in the number of degrees of loft opens up. This gap can be filled by a wedge of loft halfway between the pitching and sand wedges, called a gap wedge. Get yours checked – you may need an extra wedge.

Gimmies

A 'gimmie' is short for a 'give me', which relates to a very short putt in a friendly game (all putts must be putted out in strokeplay competitions). The player whose ball is to be putted asks his fellow player(s) if he may not putt, as his ball is so close to the hole. If they agree, he may pick up his ball, and count one stroke as if he had actually putted the ball in to the hole.

A problem with 'gimmies' is that they may not, on occasion, be given, which can be a form of gamesmanship intended to unsettle the player. Another problem is how 'close' is 'close'. Older players may remember the guideline of 'within the leather', meaning closer to the hole than the length of their putter below the grip (grips used to be leather). Another saying is "make them putt the one you wouldn't want to putt yourself".

If in doubt, decide beforehand not to give any 'gimmies': it's good practice anyway always to putt out.

Glove

Most golfers, but not all, wear a glove on their left hand, which is said to improve their grip on the club. For wet conditions, an 'all-weather' glove can be worn.

Golfcross

A game invented in New Zealand, using normal clubs to strike golf balls shaped like rugby balls into 'goals'

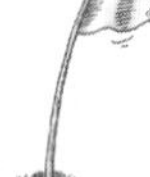

along a typical golf course layout. Instead of putting into a hole you chip the ball between two upright poles into a net. Any questions?

Grasses

The design of golf courses is very much concerned with agronomy and the various different types of grass which may be used for greens, fairways and rough, around the world. These may include fescue, bent, bermuda, kikuyu, poanna, paspalum, and so on.

Some grasses, for example bermuda, do not regrow if divots are replaced, in which case they should be filled with the appropriate 'mixture'.

Greens

Innocent-looking, beautifully mown patches of land that can turn competent, confident golfers into gibbering wrecks.

... browns, and whites

Whilst in most countries of the world, golf is played using grass greens, this is not always the case. In some desert areas, 'homesick' golfers use oil to thicken the sand for the greens, which in those places are called 'browns'. In Arctic areas, the greens are formed by scraping flat areas in the snow and ice, and these are called 'whites'.

rub of the ...

The expression 'rub of the green' refers to good

fortune or bad fortune. You may hit a very good shot which lands in a divot and shoots sideways into a bunker. You may hit a bad shot that bounces off a tree and finishes on the green. Both have to be accepted as 'rub of the green'. A fortunate bounce in the right direction is often called a 'member's bounce'.

Hacker

A hacker is a derogatory term for a bad golfer who lunges at the ball, tries to hit it too hard, and invariably makes bad shots whilst either missing the ball completely or sending divots in all directions.

Handicap Certificate

When you have gained a handicap certificate (see 2.05, Handicapping) from the Professional or Golf England, do remember to take it with you when visiting another Club, playing in a competition, or travelling abroad, as failure to do so may result in non-acceptance by the host.

Head covers

Head covers provide protection to your clubs when other clubs are returned to your golf bag. Irons may have head covers (although they are easy to lose), and head covers for woods may also have a long sleeve which is intended to protect carbon shafts from damage by iron heads.

Honour

As a general rule on the first tee, the player, or partnership, with the lowest handicap tees off first – they are said to have 'the honour'. On every other tee, the player, or partnership, who won the last hole, or had the lower score, has the honour, and tees off first.

In a Stableford competition, the higher points score assumes the honour, irrespective of the number of strokes taken by another player on the last hole.

On fairways, in the rough, or in a hazard, or on the greens, the player to play next is always the one whose ball is furthest from the hole. Sometimes a player on the green is further from the hole than someone off the green – it is his right to play, however, unless, in a friendly, the player off the green is allowed to play first. He'll then tend the flag for the long distance putter, as a concession to save time.

One of the most hated phrases in golf must surely be "it's still your turn!" after you have just putted...

In the zone

'In the zone' refers to a player who is playing well – 'one shot at a time', 'in the present', 'on a roll', 'luck is with him' are some of the many other phrases used here. It means that he is totally concentrating on his play to the exclusion of outside distractions and, as a result, achieving a good score.

Iron Byron

A machine used to test the performance of golf clubs - named after US professional Byron Nelson.

Jigger

A jigger is an iron club with a heavy head – a cross, or combination of a putter and a wedge. It is used by those who have difficulty with pitch-and-run shots onto the green from bare or tight lies.

Laying Up

A player may 'lay up' for one of two reasons. Firstly, if his ball is in trouble, he may be unable to reach the green with his next shot. He will, therefore, 'lay up', or strike his ball to a place on the fairway from where he may then have a clear shot to the green with his next stroke. Secondly, if in doubt about his ability to reach the green with his next shot due to intervening hazards – like a stream crossing the fairway – then he may 'lay up' short of the hazard, leaving himself the most acceptable yardage for his next stroke to the green.

Legs

If, after being struck, a ball looks as though it will not reach the distance required, then a player may exclaim " I don't think it has the legs!" – or something similar.

When a player says "be right", it means that he has

every confidence that the shot he has just hit will finish near the hole.

Lie

The 'lie' of the ball describes how well or badly it is positioned for the next stroke. For example, it may be in a divot, or partly covered by sand in a bunker – these would be described as 'bad' lies. If, however, the ball is 'sitting up' nicely in the fairway, this would be a 'good' lie.

A player may declare his ball 'unplayable' anywhere on the course, except in a water hazard, subject to a one-stroke penalty (Rule 28).

Lightning

In a competition, the only valid reasons for stopping play are because: the Committee has suspended play; there is danger from lightning; a decision is awaited; or through illness. Bad weather is not of itself a good reason for discontinuing play, and disqualification can result.

Lightning is extremely dangerous for golfers in view of the metal clubs carried and their isolated status on the course. For professional tournaments, advance weather warnings alert the organisers. Play is stopped if lightning is possible. The best advice seems to be to take early action; abandon clubs, etc. if caught by surprise; attempt to get into a car or building; squat low to the ground if in open space; avoid single large trees, towers, fences, telephone and power cables and poles; if in woods find an area protected by a low clump of trees; crouch with hands on knees.

If you can hear thunder, you are in danger from lightning. Counting the number of seconds between a lightning flash and thunder and dividing by 5 gives the mileage you are from the storm, but you are in danger even if the storm is not overhead.

Do not copy the foolish golfer who walked along the fairway in a thunderstorm holding a 1-iron above his head. "*What are you doing?*" asked his friend. He replied "*Well, even God can't hit a 1-iron!!!*"

Line of Sight

This usually applies to professional tournaments, where an advertising hoarding, TV tower or spectator grandstand interferes with the line of a player's next shot. Special rules apply, enabling the player to obtain relief by dropping at a point not nearer the hole, avoiding the obstruction.

Links

Links courses are near seashores. They are called 'Links' because they were originally thought of as a chain of tees and greens 'linked' together, or, by some, as sandy areas linking the seashore to the cultivated land. Other types of golf courses may be 'parkland', 'heath land', 'cliff top', etc., depending upon location.

Luck

There is a saying to the effect that neither life nor golf is fair. Certainly, luck is a big factor in golf for both professionals and amateurs. Without it, a good round is unlikely; with it, anything is possible. Remember that a scorecard paints no pictures! It's not 'how' but 'how many'.

Jack Nicklaus once said that the more he practises, the 'luckier' he gets!

Mashie

The old name for a 5-iron.

Mashie/niblick

The old name for a 7-iron.

Mulligan

'Mulligan' is the practice of allowing a first tee shot to be replayed without penalty if it proves unsatisfactory. It is not recognised in the Rules of Golf.

Niblick

The old name for a 9-iron.

Nearest point of maximum available relief

A ball shall be re-dropped without penalty if it rolls

and comes to rest nearer the hole than the nearest point of relief, or 'maximum available relief' in the situations outlined in the next paragraph. If complete relief is not possible in a bunker or on a green, a player may drop the ball at the nearest point of maximum available relief (i.e. without a one club-length dropping area) but not nearer the hole.

Nearest point of relief

The point on the course nearest to where the ball lies, but which is not nearer the hole, and at which if the ball were positioned there would be no interference to the player's swing or stance, is the nearest point of relief. It usually applies to players facing immovable obstructions, abnormal ground conditions, a wrong putting green, or staked trees.

Old Man's Persuader

Some players, when putting, extend their forefinger down the shaft of the putter. This is called the 'old man's persuader' or the 'old gentleman's persuader'.

Outside Agency

Anything which is not part of the match, including referees, observers, birds, foxes, etc. See Rule 18.

Over/underclubbing

To 'overclub' or to 'take too much club' both mean

that you have hit the ball too far because you have chosen a club with too little loft – perhaps a 6-iron instead of a 7-iron. Similarly, to 'underclub' or 'take too little club' mean that you haven't hit it far enough – perhaps you used a 4-iron instead of a 3-iron?

Pin High

'Pin High' is an expression which, in modern times, means that the length of a shot is correct but poor direction leaves the ball to one side of the hole, either on or off the green.

Pitchmarks

When a ball lands on a green from a high trajectory, it breaks the grass surface and leaves an indentation. It is every player's duty to find their pitchmark (ball mark) or confirm that none was made, and repair it with a repairer (on sale in the Pro's shop). If this is done immediately, a pitchmark can recover in 24 hours. If left, it will require the greenkeeper's attention and take much longer, thus causing problems for any player who has to putt across it – this may be you!

It is good practice to repair your own pitchmark, and at least one other, on every green you play. A ball embedded in its own pitchmark in any 'closely mown' area through the green may be lifted, cleaned and dropped without penalty as near as possible to the spot where it lay, but not nearer the hole.

Play-off

A competition may require that an outright champion is declared, as opposed to joint-winners. Competitions vary – some require that four extra holes be played, or even 18. Some specify 'sudden death', whereby the first player to win an extra hole is declared the winner.

Plus-fours

Plus-fours are trousers terminating 4 inches below the knee. Plus-twos terminate 2 inches below the knee. Not quite as popular on the course as they once were.

Pre-shot routine

Before making a stroke, including a putt on the putting green, it is considered good practice to follow a set routine. This may include standing a few paces behind the ball, visualising the flight or path of the ball, placing the club behind the ball, placing the feet in position and even breathing in a certain way. This routine, if carried out every time, is said to concentrate the mind and avoid 'panic' in times of stress. Whatever you decide to do, make sure it doesn't take too long or you will be criticised.

Preferred Lies

Often called 'Winter Rules,' preferred lies are sanctioned by many Clubs throughout the Winter period, especially where courses are subject to very wet conditions. Clubs should be very specific about the details to be observed (see ROG App.1 Part B.3b). The concession usually allows players to mark, lift and clean their ball when on the fairway, and then to replace it within 6 inches of its marked position, though not nearer the hole. Players should not become lax about moving their ball without first marking its position with a tee peg, especially if it's a winter competition. Preferred lies apply to closely mown areas (cut to fairway height or less) only, and not to the rough. Sometimes in severe conditions, or prior to a prestigious tournament, a Club may require that the ball is actually placed on a tee peg or on a mat on the fairway.

Press

A press is the forward movement of the hands immediately prior to making a backswing and playing a stroke. Some players employ this action as they feel it initiates the backswing in a smooth, controlled manner. Others 'hover' the clubhead above ground level before takeaway.

Pro-Am

Frequently, in advance of a Tour event or as a special Club event, there will be a Pro-Am or Pro-Celebrity Day, when professional players team up with amateurs to play a round of golf, the proceeds of which are given to charity.

Punch shot

Nothing to do with swinging a fist! A punch shot is a low forcing shot, perhaps passing under the branches of a tree. It is achieved by taking a less lofted club, keeping the ball back in the stance, shortening the grip, and executing a shot where the backswing and the follow-through are of equal length and foreshortened to about shoulder height.

It is a shot often used when backspin is not required.

Putt

Don't say that word to me!

clutch ...

When under pressure and the leading scores are close, a clutch putt is one that must go in.

lag ...

Normally, a long putt which is intended to finish so near to the hole that only a short 'stone dead' putt is required to hole out.

...ing out.

When, in a Stableford competition, a player has amassed more strokes at a hole than can earn him any points, he should pick up his ball and proceed to the next tee without delay. For example: if a player is to receive one stroke on a par 4, he has to score a six to earn one point. If he plays 6 strokes and has still not holed out, he should pick up the ball and move on. If a player receives 2 strokes on a par 4, he has to score

7 to earn one point. If he plays 7 and has still not holed out, he should pick up and avoid delay.

'Q' School

Professional golfers seeking their 'card' to play in European Tour events may achieve this by either amassing sufficient earnings on the 'Challenge' Tour, or by playing six rounds of golf at a 'Q' or 'Qualifying School' at the end of the season. A certain number of players will, as a result, receive their Tour cards for the following year.

Rabbit

A 'rabbit' is a novice or beginner.

Raking bunkers

When a player has completed his stroke(s) out of a bunker, he must rake the disturbed sand with the rake provided. Failure to do so means that the ball of a following player might well land in your footprints. It might be your ball in someone else's footprints next time... Etiquette dictates that you always rake the bunkers before leaving a bunker, even if others are remiss.

The R & A recommends that rakes be left outside bunkers, but many courses require that they be left inside. You need to know the policy of the course you are playing.

Redan

The name of the par 3 15th hole at the North Berwick Golf Club, West Links. The hole is well known for its design, which features a green on top of a plateau with bunkers front right and left. Also the name of a similar par 3 at Shinnecock Hills, where the 2004 US Open was played.

Relaxation

The best advice given, but the most difficult to follow, is to relax whilst swinging a golf club. Any anxiety translates into a tight grip, which makes the arms and shoulders tight, which in turn inhibits a smooth swing and results in a poor shot. A golf swing should be slow and easy, with good tempo and rhythm.

Self-policing

Golf is one of the only games in the world in which players keep their own scores (subject to checks), and are trusted to police themselves with regard to the application of etiquette and rules. This tradition has been built up over many years, and is guarded jealously. It is the envy of other sportsmen worldwide, and all players are expected to abide by it.

Shotgun start

Some competitions require that all players commence playing at the same time, so that, at tee-off time, there are groups of players on all 18 tees (subject to the number of entrants). To start them off, traditionally a shotgun has been fired somewhere nearby, where all the players can hear it, but this practice is dying out in favour of a siren or hooter. This form of competition ensures that all the players complete their rounds at more or less the same time.

Slope Index

In many countries the 'Slope Index' is a method of adjusting players' handicaps in accordance with a formula to reflect the degree of difficulty of a course, thus making them more representative of visiting golfers' abilities. It can be thought of as your handicap for the day for the particular course that you are playing.

Spitting

Spitting on the course is considered in the UK to be a disgusting habit. However, some countries still consider it to be part of their culture, and frequent examples can be seen on TV, to the extent that the Rules have been employed to deal with spittle on the playing surface as 'casual water'.

PLEASE do not do it! It is horrible, disgusting, degrading, quite unnecessary and a very bad example to Junior golfers.

Spoon

The old name for a 3-wood.

Stance

Your stance is when you place your feet in position to play a stroke. Normally, your toes will be on a line parallel to the target line (the line from the ball to where you want it to land). In an 'open' stance, the left foot is drawn back (usually for wedge shots where the ball is positioned nearer the right heel). In a 'closed' stance, the right foot is drawn back (usually for woods or long irons, or to encourage a 'draw', where the ball is positioned nearer the left heel.)

You must not 'build' a stance, e.g. kneel on a towel or stand on a buggy.

Start time

It is common courtesy to your playing partners, and other players, to be ready to start at the allotted, or booked, tee-time.

However, for a competition, if you are late you will be disqualified. You have been warned!

Stimpmeter

The speed at which a ball rolls across a green will depend upon many factors, not least of which are the type of grass, its length, and the evenness of the

surface. In order to specify the quality of putting surface required, a method of measurement has been devised using a piece of equipment called a 'stimpmeter.' This is an 'L' shaped metal bar, approximately three feet long, one end of which is placed on a level part of the green. A golf ball is placed next to a raised 'notch' at the other end, and the bar is raised until the ball is released from the 'notch', runs down the bar and across the green. The distance it travels across the green is then measured, in feet. The procedure is repeated on the same area of the green, but in the opposite direction, and an average of the two distances is calculated. The resulting measurement is called the 'stimpmeter' reading, and will vary from about 8 to 10 feet for normal courses, and from 11 to 12 feet for championship courses. So, the higher the reading, the slicker the greens. The stimpmeter bar is identical worldwide, so that accurate comparisons can be made.

Stretch

'Down the stretch' is a term applied to the last 9 holes of a competition, when the pressure and excitement are at their highest.

Strokesavers (or similar name)

A booklet produced by many course managers giving a diagram of each hole, and the yardages from various objects on the course to the green. It's ideal for visitors to a course.

Stymie

Before the RULES OF GOLF were changed to permit marking and lifting of a ball on the green, it used to be that balls on the green had to be played as they lay, even if one player's ball was on his opponent's line (by accident or intent!). A ball which was thus blocked from a direct route to the hole was said to be 'stymied'.

Sweet spot

The face of a clubhead makes contact with the ball. There is said to be a 'sweet spot' on all clubhead faces, being the contact point between club and ball which will give the best results in terms of accuracy, length and consistency. Cavity-backed heads with peripheral weighting are said to have a larger 'sweet spot' than bladed clubs. Large-headed drivers are also said to have an increased 'sweet spot' area.

If you bounce a ball on a clubhead face, you can determine, by sound and feel, where the sweet spot is located. By powdering the face and making a stroke, you can see where the contact point with the ball was actually made.

The sweet spot theory applies to putters as well as woods and irons.

Swing weight

One of the properties of a golf club, which a Professional will measure when assessing its suitability for a potential buyer, is its swing weight. Categories such as C8, D1, D4, etc. are calculated by consideration of the weight of the individual clubhead and its shaft. Professional players will ensure that all of their clubs conform to their desired swing weight, in order to improve consistency and their 'feel' for each club. Other measurements taken include matched flexibility and the lie angle of the shafts.

Tee Box

Often, the marked teeing ground is referred to as the 'tee box'. Historically, however, the tee box was the box, containing sand, placed alongside the teeing ground. Before tee pegs were invented, the sand was used by players to form a mound, upon which the ball was placed before teeing off.

Tee Pegs

Tee pegs are produced in many shapes, sizes and colours. The colours are immaterial, except that green or brown ones may be difficult to see in grass, the same applying to white ones in the snow. Ideally, bio-degradable or wooden pegs should be used. Even if playing irons off the tee, you are recommended to use a tee peg at ground level for better ball-striking.

The height of the ball above ground level when teed

may vary depending upon various factors (See 3.01). When using a (metal) wood, it is generally advised that half the ball, when teed, is showing above the top of the clubhead when placed on the ground. In the case of the shaped 'castle' tees, usually a yellow or white one is used with a driver (1-wood), a blue one with a 3-wood, and red ones for 5-wood or irons.

Latest developments include brush tees, various biodegradable tees, laser line tees (offset), flying tees (pincers), Willit tees (two pronged), rubber-headed tees, lift tees and adjustable tees. There are even tees available which, when snapped on impact, may reveal that the player has won a prize!

Through the green

'Through the green' is the whole area of the course except teeing grounds, putting greens and hazards.

Tiger line

A 'Tiger line' refers to a difficult shot which, although direct to the green, may involve crossing bunkers, water or trees, etc. The alternative would be to play 'safe', or lay up.

TPC

'Tour Players' Courses' are certain courses designated as such on the American Tour and designed to hold professional tournaments. Their layouts usually include suitable 'banking' to facilitate spectator viewing.

TPC can also refer to Tournament Players' Championship, played once a year and considered by many to be the fifth Major.

Up and down

If a ball is off the green – maybe even in a bunker – a player is deemed to have 'got up and down' if he plays the ball onto the green with his next shot, and holes out with his next shot.

Warm-up

Golf may not be an aerobic activity (although there are many stories to disprove this!), but it is certainly an athletic pursuit. Players should always prepare themselves before playing by taking exercise – gentle if necessary – to loosen joints and muscles. There is nothing worse than straining muscles on a very cold winter's morning just because one is too lazy to warm up. If nothing else, try to swing two iron clubs together for a few minutes.

A player should ideally arrive in time to familiarise himself with his surroundings, pay green fees, obtain card, check the weather, meet partners/opponents, etc, in addition to warming up in the nets and spending time on the practice putting green. How often do we see a player roar into the car park, boot open, shoes on, grabbing his clubs and heading straight onto the first tee? Then he wonders why he duffs his drive and sprains his back!

Widow

A 'golf widow' is a non-golfing lady married to a golfer, so called because she is deserted for long periods whilst her husband is playing golf. It is noted that little mention is ever made of a 'golf widower'!

Winter Rules

See 'Preferred lies'.

Yips

This is a condition which primarily refers to a player's inability to putt his ball. It may manifest itself as an inability, having addressed the ball, to take the putter away and hit the ball. It may be an uncontrollable twitch or jerk. Players with this affliction are usually counselled, and frequently find an alternative grip on the putter or long-shafted club which may give some control.

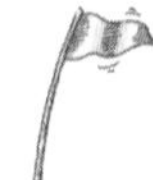

EPILOGUE

We all know that once the 'golfing bug' bites, it's very tenacious. Recently a golfer with a furrowed brow asked me how he could give up the game. I imagine this question was prompted by his last round.

The question is a difficult one to answer. Mentally we can convince ourselves that we should give up because we are no good at it, have no chance of getting better, have never won anything and are unlikely ever to do so. Also it's too time-consuming (there's decorating to be done!) and it's too costly, even if more lessons might help!

On the physical front we are losing length off the tee, easy putts no longer drop, our partners take too long and winter golf only highlights the aches and pains waiting to rack our rapidly deteriorating bodies!

So, how do we accept all these home truths and make a final decision to give it all up, and not play "just one more round, so that I will not let my friends down you understand!" It will not work and you know it!

You either have to lose your marbles completely and be

locked up, or become physically incapable – a very hard thing to do as even legless, armless and blind people all play golf, not to mention courses 'overflowing' with injured golfers.

I'm afraid it will only end when the Grim Reaper repairs your very last divot and places a headstone on it. And if you go to Hell, remember that there will be beautiful golf courses there with excellent facilities, shops with shoes, clothing, bags and buggies and a wonderful array of clubs – all free! But there are no golf balls!

Golf is not easy, golf is not fair. At whatever level you play the game, to 'improve' gives the greatest satisfaction that this intriguing sport can offer.

So, my answer to the hapless golfer's original question – "You can't!"

See you on the first tee!

Strive, achieve, enjoy.

PMW 2004.

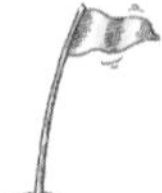

Some useful addresses

English Golf Union
www.englishgolfunion.org | info@englishgolfunion.org
tel 01526 354500; fax 01526 354020

Golf England tel 0870 243 2343 www.golfengland.com
<http://www.golfengland.com>

Golfing Union of Ireland Donneybrook, Dublin.
www.gui.ie | information@gui.ie | tel 353(0)12694111.

Scottish Golf Union St Andrews
www.scottishgolfunion.org/ | sgu@scottishgolfunion.org
tel 01382 549 500.

Welsh Golfing Union Newport, Gwent
www.welshgolf.org | wgu@welshgolf.org | tel 01633 430 830

Ladies Golf Union (LGU) St Andrews
www.lgu.org/ | info@lgu.org | tel 01334 475 811

English Ladies Golf Association (ELGA) Birmingham
www.englishladiesgolf.org | office@englishladiesgolf.org
tel 01214 562 088.

Golf Foundation Hertfordshire
www.golf-foundation.org
communications@golf-foundation.org | tel 01920 876 200

National Association of Public Golf Courses
www.NAPGC.org.uk | tel 01527 542 106

Club Secretaries may contact The National Golf Clubs Advisory Association for legal or administrative advice - tel 01684 311 353.

INDEX

INDEX